Best Easy Day Hikes Series

Best Easy Day Hikes
Boise

Natalie L. Bartley

D0818600

FALCONGUIDES

GUILFORD, CONNECTICUT
HELENA, MONTANA

Project editor: Gregory Hyman
Layout: Kevin Mak
Maps: OffRoute Inc. © Rowman & Littlefield

Library of Congress Cataloging-in-Publication Data is available on file.

ISBN 978-0-7627-5271-3

Printed in the United States of America

Distributed by NATIONAL BOOK NETWORK

Contents

Acknowledgments.. vi

Introduction.. 1

How to Use This Guide 13

Map Legend.. 15

Trail Finder.. 16

The Hikes

1. Oregon Trail Historic Reserve Trail System 19
2. Boise River Greenbelt: Bethine
   Church River Trail 23
3. Table Rock to Old Idaho State
   Penitentiary Trails.. 28
4. Hulls Gulch Interpretive Trail 33
5. Veterans Memorial Park: Boise
   Cascade Lake Loop... 38
6. Corrals Trail: Miller Gulch Trailhead
   to Corrals–Bogus Basin Road Trailhead.................... 43
7. Polecat Gulch Reserve: Polecat Loop Trail............... 47
8. Hidden Springs: Red Tail and
   Lookout Loop Trails 52
9. Garden City Greenbelt Pathway:
   River Pointe Park Nature Trail................................... 56
10. Garden City Greenbelt Pathway:
    Riverside Pedestrian Path 60
11. Reid W. Merrill Sr. Community Park:
    Eagle Pathways.. 64
12. Avimor: Burnt Car
    Draw Trail.. 68
13. Kuna: Indian Creek Greenbelt 72

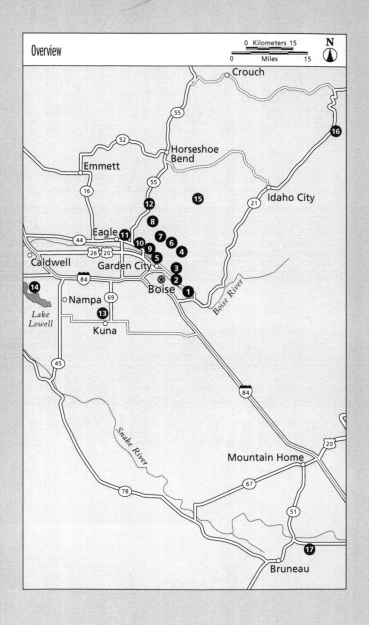

Overview

0 Kilometers 15
0 Miles 15

N

Crouch

55

52

Emmett

Horseshoe
Bend

16

55

12

15

Idaho City

21

Eagle

44

11

8

7

6

4

10

9

26 20

Caldwell

Garden City

5

84

3

2

Boise

1

Boise River

14

Lake
Lowell

Nampa

69

13

45

Kuna

84

Snake River

Mountain Home

20

78

67

51

17

Bruneau

14. Deer Flat National Wildlife Refuge:
    Nature Trail Habitat Hike 76
15. Boise National Forest: Mores Mountain
    Interpretive Trail Extension...................................... 81
16. Boise National Forest:
    Crooked River Trail 87
17. Bruneau Dunes State Park: Big Dune Hike 91

Hiking and Outdoor Clubs... 96
About the Author 97

Acknowledgments

Kudos and hugs go to my friends and relatives who traveled the highways and trails with me and read or followed the hike descriptions developed for this guidebook. Heartfelt thanks go to the various land managers and agency representatives for their share in adding to this guide's usability through reviewing their specific trails.

Thank you also to the helpful staff at DeLorme Publishing Company, Inc., for their assistance with Global Positioning System (GPS) questions. Last but not least, a big thanks to the staff at Globe Pequot Press, including acquisition editor Scott Adams, the cartographers, copy editors, design artists, production staff, and many others who made this guidebook a reality.

Introduction

Selecting the seventeen best easy day hikes in Boise and the vicinity is an exciting yet challenging task. From the forested mountains and the lush river valley to the surrounding high desert of the Snake River plain, there are so many outstanding choices within a 60-mile drive of Idaho's capital city.

The present-day drainage system of the Boise River, with cities lining its banks and the swath of agricultural land between Mountain Home to the east and Payette near the Idaho-Oregon border to the west, is commonly known as the Treasure Valley. Boise and the surrounding areas are fringed by federal public land managed by the Boise National Forest and the Bureau of Land Management.

Trails in the City of Boise's Boise River Greenbelt system are noteworthy for their convenience and tranquility. City managers had the foresight to protect the river corridor for future use as a public trail system. The Boise River Greenbelt stands as a role model for Idaho urban trail systems. Additionally, the cities of Boise, Garden City, and Eagle each have a system of greenbelt pathways along the banks of the Boise River. Toss in city, county, and state public land, and the hiking possibilities bloom.

Numerous property-access agreements with private landowners in the Boise foothills helped create the Ridge to Rivers Trail System. Consisting of more than 125 miles of public-use trails on 80,000 acres of land, the trails are easily accessed from various trailheads along the Boise foothills near Boise.

Included in the Ridge to Rivers Trail System are two nationally designated trails. The Oregon Trail Historic

Reserve Trail System is part of the 2,170-mile Oregon National Historic Trail. Hulls Gulch Interpretive Trail, a pedestrian-only trail, is a designated National Recreation Trail.

Geology strongly defines the Treasure Valley. Eight to nine million years ago a lake, named Lake Idaho by geologists, formed between the Boise Ridge to the north and the Owyhee Mountains to the south. The old lake was nearly 35 miles wide and 200 miles long. Indications of the lake are clearly visible from vantage points high above the vast valley. Various layers of volcanic and lake sediments consisting of sand, clay, and pebble remain today. These materials, carried in by river activity and deposited in Lake Idaho, reached greater than 4,000 feet in thickness.

The north edge of the Boise Ridge comprises granodiorite of the Idaho Batholith, with an overlay of volcanic rocks and boulder gravel. Shafer Butte, the highest point in the Boise Ridge, was created by a fault in the area that raised the rocks in the east side of the valley and tipped the rocks downward in the western part of the valley.

Not only is the geology readily visible, it is part of the everyday vocabulary of trail users. During each spring, when vegetation is prolific, cattle and hikers share the draw—a shallow gully. After a steep uphill climb, hikers step onto a saddle, the low area connecting two higher points on the ridge. Emigrants on the Oregon Trail were desperate to find a way off the bench—a flat, elevated piece of land also called a terrace—to the lush river valley below.

Benches in Boise and to the south of the valley were once the bottom of the old lake. They were formed by repetitive glacial growth and melting, excavating the valley. There are several benches in the Treasure Valley. Outlying perimeter benches contain basalt. Other benches are within or near the Boise River's hundred-year floodplain.

Hikers in the foothills tread on the edge of the old shoreline of the lake while viewing the extensive valley and benches below. Stand atop Table Rock, the remains of the bottom of the long-lost lake. Learn more about the geology of the Treasure Valley at the Idaho Museum of Mining and Geology, next to the Old Idaho State Penitentiary near the Table Rock–Old Penitentiary trailhead.

The trails described in this book provide a sampling of the endless number of hiking options in the Boise vicinity. Shaded hikes on smooth paved trails along the glittering Boise River or upland hikes through sagebrush with stunning valley views represent just a few of the options. Discover sand dunes, mountain streams, or historical wagon train trails. It is all there for modern-day explorers.

Weather

Boise is famous for its high-desert climate with steady sunshine, 230 days per year, and low-humidity averaging near 30 percent in summer. Annual rainfall averages 12 inches, with the majority of precipitation occurring October through March.

Winters are often moderate in town, with snow remaining on the ground only for a day or two. In the mountains, snow falls from October through May and is usually associated with foggy conditions. Fog frequents the valley from late November through mid-February during times of temperature inversions. Higher elevation trails in the foothills and the trails beyond Boise enable hikers to get above the inversion for a shot of sunshine.

July is the hottest month in the Treasure Valley, with average daytime temperatures around 90 degrees Fahrenheit and nighttime lows around 62 degrees. In general, plan for hot weather on Boise foothills hikes during late spring, summer, and early fall. On the hottest days, temperatures can hit 100 degrees by midday and remain hot until late evening after the sun goes down. Temperatures can be even hotter during heat waves, soaring as high as 105 degrees.

Spring and autumn months are cooler for hiking, as are early-summer mornings. Come January, the coldest month, daytime temperatures average about 32 degrees, with nighttime lows around 22 degrees.

Localized thunderstorms are a weather hazard in the Boise foothills during late spring and summer. Short, intense precipitation combined with the foothills' steep terrain can lead to flash flooding of creeks and streams in the basins. Check the weather reports before setting off on hikes or select an alternate trail, perhaps along the Boise River, where flows are dam controlled.

While on mountain trails, be prepared for variable weather, including cool weather and the possibility of thunderstorms, which can develop quickly. On rare occasions, brief snow showers are possible in the high mountains in midsummer.

To learn more about local weather, visit www.weather.gov/Boise. This handy Web site allows you to zoom in on the location of the trails for a detailed weather report. The Boise National Weather Service Forecast Office sends out warnings on extreme weather conditions and related hazards via television, National Oceanic and Atmospheric Administration (NOAA) weather radio, and the Internet.

Safety and Preparation

Many of the trails in this guide are multiuse. Hikers may be sharing the area with mountain bikers, trail runners, equestrians, and all-terrain or four-wheel-drive motorized vehicles. Adhering to the following "Rules of the Road" will help all trail users have a pleasant and safe outdoor experience.

- Keep to the right side of the path when others are passing by.
- Pass slower folks by moving to the left to go by them.
- Control children and pets while on the trail, and be sure to pack out pet wastes.
- When encountering equestrians, speak to them so the horse knows you are human.
- Be sure to pack out everything carried in, keeping the trail litter-free for future users.

You can usually hike year-round in the Boise foothills. During winter, trails freeze overnight and are still firm in the early morning, thus low impact to walk on. Temporary trail closures occur when ground moisture is excessive and trail damage could occur, typically during late winter and early spring. If the trails are wet and muddy, go somewhere else to hike, such as the paved Boise River Greenbelt. The land in the foothills is fragile, and using the tracks in wet conditions leaves them rutted and eroded. In the future, land managers may consider limiting trail use to the early-morning hours during the freeze-thaw cycles.

Though hiking in the Boise area is physically and mentally beneficial, there are a few health and safety considerations. In late summer, smoke from forest fires in Idaho and surrounding states find its way to the Treasure Valley. During winter, as is typical in other metropolitan areas, temperature inversions occur. Air quality warnings are posted in the newspapers and reported on the radio and on television. Consider the air quality ratings when planning hikes.

In the summer and autumn, fire restrictions are posted at trailheads during dry conditions, particularly in the foothills and the mountains. Please refrain from smoking cigarettes, setting off fireworks, or starting campfires during fire-restricted times.

Dress in layers for variable weather conditions. The layer closest to the body is generally a perspiration-wicking layer, followed by an insulating layer for warmth. A wind-breaking outer layer helps add warmth in windy conditions, and a rain-shedding outer layer keeps you dry in wet conditions. The beauty of the layering system is the ability to add or subtract layers during the hike, maintaining a comfortable body temperature and protection from the elements. Proper footwear, such as sneakers designed for trail walking or light hiking boots, is essential.

Clear, sunny days—even hazy ones—can lead to sunburn. Remember to slather on a broad-spectrum UVB/ UVA protective sunscreen. Reapply every few hours, after sweating, and after swimming. Bring plenty of water; the low-humidity air contributes to rapid fluid loss, as do high temperatures.

While hiking in the Boise foothills, you might encounter ticks. Consider wearing long pants to keep ticks off your legs during spring and early summer. Check your dog for ticks as well.

Rattlesnakes and nonpoisonous snakes are relatively common, particularly on rocky trails when the day heats up. Hikers usually see the snakes quickly slithering away, avoiding contact with humans. Make plenty of noise, look before you step, and leave the snakes alone.

Deer, elk, and coyotes are often sighted in the foothills. They are shy creatures and avoid hikers. Bears and mountain lions inhabit some of the higher elevation public lands in the area, although encounters are unlikely.

Zero Impact

Trails in the Ridge to River Trail System and surrounding areas are increasingly popular. Trail users assure the ongoing quality of and existence of trails by following Zero Impact guidelines to lessen human impact on the trails. Here are some basic trail preservation guidelines:

- Pack out all trash generated during the hike, including biodegradable items such as apple cores. Consider packing out other trash left behind by less-considerate users.
- Do not approach or feed wildlife.
- Leave wildflowers, rocks, antlers, feathers, and other historic and natural objects for other hikers to enjoy. In some cases it may be illegal to remove such items.
- Avoid damaging trailside soils and plants by remaining on the designated trail.
- Refrain from using or creating switchbacks and short cuts, which promote erosion.
- Be courteous by not making loud noises while hiking.

- When on a multiuse trail shared with mountain bikers, trail runners, and equestrians, familiarize yourself with proper trail etiquette, yielding the trail when appropriate.
- Use the outhouses at trailheads and along the trail.

Public Land Management

Occupying a prominent position in the Treasure Valley landscape is the Boise Front, consisting of the foothills leading into Boise National Forest. Visionary land-use planners designated, mapped, and publicized the numerous trail opportunities known today as the Ridge to Rivers Trail System. Initiated in 1992 as a future-oriented, multi-agency trail plan, the trail system received a strong boost with the passing of the Boise Foothills Levy in 2000. The levy provides funding for buying land for open space for wildlife habitat and for trails.

This unique partnership between governmental agencies, nonprofit organizations, and private landowners creates dynamic and growing recreational trail opportunities for residents and visitors alike. The trail system serves as the centerpiece for hiking in the Boise area.

Trails invite exploration into the various ecosystems, ranging from the Boise River in the valley floor at 2,500 feet elevation to the Boise Ridge mountaintops at 7,582 feet. The Shafer Butte Trail System in Boise National Forest is part of the Ridge to Rivers Trail System and has a separate map.

You can purchase both maps at local outdoor retail shops or view the trails online at www.ridgetorivers.org. Each map provides an excellent overview of the trail system and terrain, with aerial photographs on one side and a three-dimensional overview of the trails on the other side. Numerous hiking, biking, and horse riding trails grace the designated trails in Military Reserve, Camel's Back Park and Hulls Gulch Reserve, Table Rock and Castle Rock Reserves, and Shafer Butte.

Hikers using the Ridge to Rivers Trail System pass through private property on some of the trails. Ranchers graze sheep or cattle here during part of the year. The trail system management has agreements with the landowners for trail use. Trail users need to do their part by being respectful of private property and following the trail rules.

If you encounter a flock of domestic sheep, you may see Great Pyrenees or Akbash dogs accompanying them. These dogs are trained for livestock protection. Stay clear of the flock and make the animals aware of your presence by speaking to them. Move slowly so as not to alarm the sheep or the dogs. Keep your pet leashed and controlled.

You may encounter sheep or cattle on the Corrals Trail and Hulls Gulch Interpretive Trail described in this guide. For more information visit the Idaho Rangeland Resource Commission at www.idahorange.org or call (877) ID-Range (437-2643). Alternatively, pick up a *Care for Idaho's Rangelands—Share Them Respectfully with Others* pamphlet at Ridge to Rivers Trail System trailhead kiosks.

The popularity of hiking with pets has grown steadily, along with the valley's population. For continued enjoyment of hiking with their four-footed friends, trail users need to adhere to the pet regulations enforced in the Ridge to Rivers Trail System. Dog owners are required to carry a leash and "mutt mitts" for waste disposal at all times. The plastic bags are available at various trailheads, where you should also deposit the wastes in the provided trashcans.

Some trails are specifically designated on-leash, and dogs need to remain on-leash while on these trails. On designated off-leash trails, dogs must be under voice control and within 30 feet of the hiker. Volunteer and paid trail patrollers educate users on trail rules and enforce the rules. The Idaho Humane Society also patrols trails and issues citations as necessary.

Trails in this guide go beyond the Ridge to Rivers Trail System. Additional agency and organizations managing the other trails include the USDA Forest Service; Idaho Department of Parks and Recreation; Deer Flat Wildlife Refuge; the cities of Kuna, Boise, Garden City, and Eagle; and the Avimor–SunCor development.

Boise-area trails are rapidly expanding and improving. Contact the appropriate agencies for updated information on their trails and other services in their jurisdiction.

Ridge to Rivers Trail System: Agency Partners Contact Information

The following organizations can provide further information about the hikes and trails in their service areas.

- **Ridge to Rivers Trail System,** Boise City Parks and Recreation, 3188 Sunset Peak Rd., Boise 83702; (208) 514-3756; www.ridgetorivers.org. This department coordinates the trail system. Check the Web site for current trail closures, trail maps, trail descriptions, and rules.

- **Boise City Parks and Recreation,** 1104 Royal Blvd., Boise 83706; (208) 384-4240; www.cityofboise.org/ parks. City of Boise serves as the lead agency for management of the Boise River Greenbelt through Boise and manages Boise city parks along the Greenbelt.

- **Bureau of Land Management,** Boise District Office, 3948 Development Ave., Boise 83705; (208) 384-3300; www.blm.gov.
- **USDA Forest Service,** Boise National Forest Supervisor's Office, 1249 South Vinnell Way, Suite 200, Boise 83709; (208) 373-4100; www.fs.fed.us/r4/boise.
- **Mountain Home Ranger District,** Boise National Forest, 2180 American Legion Blvd., Mountain Home 83647; (208) 587-7961; www.fs.fed.us/r4/boise.
- **Idaho City Ranger District,** Boise National Forest, 3833 ID 21, Idaho City 83631; (208) 392-6681; www.fs.fed.us/r4/boise.
- **Ada County Parks and Recreation,** 4049 Eckert Rd., Boise 83716; (208) 577-4575; www.adaweb.net.
- **Idaho Department of Fish and Game,** 600 South Walnut Ave., Boise 83712; (208)334-3700; www.fishandgame.idaho.gov. Contact them for fishing license information.
- **Old Idaho State Penitentiary,** 2445 Old Penitentiary Rd., Boise 83712; (208) 334-2844; www.idahohistory.net. Open Memorial Day to Labor Day 10:00 a.m. to 5:00 p.m.; open noon to 5:00 p.m. the rest of the year. Tours available for a small fee.

Additional Trail Agency Contacts

- **Deer Flat National Wildlife Refuge,** 13751 Upper Embankment Rd., Nampa 83686; (208) 467-9278; www.fws.gov/deerflat.
- **Idaho Department of Parks and Recreation,** 5657 Warm Springs Ave., Boise 83716; (208) 334-4199; www

.parksandrecreation.idaho.gov. Information regarding any of the thirty Idaho state parks.

- **City of Garden City,** City Hall, 6015 Glenwood St., Garden City 83714; (208) 472-2900; www.gardencity idaho.govoffice.com. Contact them for updates regarding trails along the Garden City segment of the Boise River.

- **City of Eagle,** Eagle City Hall, 660 East Civic Lane, Eagle 83616; (208) 939-6813; www.cityofeagle.org. Get updates on trail improvements in Eagle along the Boise River and surrounding areas.

- **City of Kuna,** City Hall, 763 West Avalon St., Kuna 83634; (208) 922-5546; www.cityofkuna.com. Contact them regarding parks and trails in Kuna.

- **Avimor–SunCor**, Sales Office, 18454 North McLeod Way, Boise 83714; (208) 939-5360; www.avimor.com. Provides current information on trails in the area and on the development's property.

How to Use This Guide

Designed for quick and simple usage, this guide gives hikers the basic information needed for exploring Boise's extensive trail systems. Every hike detailed here includes a brief description, hike specifications regarding distance, approximate hiking time, trail difficulty, trail surface, best seasons for enjoying the trail, other trail users, canine compatibility, fees and permits required, trail schedule, map sources, trail contacts, and special considerations. Specific directions for getting to the trail and a map diagramming the general route, access roads, and points of interest are included. A narrative describes interesting aspects of the trail ranging from history to the wildlife and wildflowers in the area. A detailed mileage description (Miles and Directions) identifies important trail junctions and landmarks on the route.

Hike Selection

Local residents may discover new trails in this guide, while out-of-towners can access Boise and vicinity hiking opportunities with confidence. Routes vary in length from 0.5 mile to 7.0 miles out and back. Difficulty is geared toward easy to moderate, though a few more challenging hikes are included. From level, paved terrain to steep, rocky trails, families with young children and experienced hikers alike will find hikes in this guide to meet their needs. Many of the described hikes include trail options extending beyond the described segments. The optional extensions are identified in the Miles and Directions sections and on the maps.

Difficulty Ratings

The seventeen trails selected for this guidebook are generally easy. With the exception of hikes along the Boise River, Crooked River, and Indian Creek, hiking in Boise and the vicinity generally includes some elevation gain and loss. From the base of the Boise foothills, the only way to go is up. Trails tend to be gentle or contain established trail switchbacks, with plenty of views of the valley as a reason to pause and rest.

Trail descriptions include a "Difficulty" rating of easy, moderate, or more challenging and offer a brief explanation for the rating. These ratings are subjective, based on the author's, readers', and hikers' unique perspectives. When selecting a hike, consider your personal fitness level, time, and the route.

- **Easy** hikes are short, along smooth surfaces, and take an hour or less to complete.
- **Moderate** hikes are generally those with longer distances and slight uphills, taking one to two hours to hike.
- **More challenging** hikes involve occasional steep and rocky sections, longer distances, and may take more than two hours to finish.

Approximate hiking times suggested in this guide are based on an average of 2 miles per hour. Timelines vary, depending on the size of the group, individual fitness levels, number of rest stops, and side explorations. Allow additional time for enjoying trailside pursuits such as bird watching, photography, reading interpretive signs, and snacking.

Map Legend

84	Interstate Highway
16	State Highway
FS374	Local/Forest Road
– – – – –	Unpaved Road
▬▬▬▬▬	Featured Trail
- - - - -	Trail
⊢–⊢–⊢–⊣	Railroad
⬭	Body of Water
～～～	River/Creek
🛥	Boat Launch
⌣	Bridge
⛺	Camping
⊛	Capital
●–●	Gate
❓	Information Center
🅿	Parking
▲	Peak
⛱	Picnic Area
■	Point of Interest/Structure
🛉	Restroom
○	Town
11	Trailhead
🖼	Viewpoint/Overlook
≳	Waterfall
∬	Rapids

Trail Finder

Best Hikes for River Lovers

 10   Garden City Greenbelt Pathway: Riverside Pedestrian Path

 11   Reid W. Merrill Sr. Community Park: Eagle Pathways

 13   Kuna: Indian Creek Greenbelt

 16   Boise National Forest: Crooked River Trail

Best Hikes for Lake Lovers

  5   Veterans Memorial Park: Boise Cascade Lake Loop

 14   Deer Flat National Wildlife Refuge: Nature Trail Habitat Hike

 17   Bruneau Dunes State Park: Big Dune Hike

Best Hikes for Autumn Colors

  4   Hulls Gulch Interpretive Trail

 15   Boise National Forest: Mores Mountain Interpretive Trail Extension

 16   Boise National Forest: Crooked River Trail

Best Hikes for Children

  5   Veterans Memorial Park: Boise Cascade Lake Loop

  9   Garden City Greenbelt Pathway: River Pointe Park Nature Trail

 11   Reid W. Merrill Sr. Community Park: Eagle Pathways

 13   Kuna: Indian Creek Greenbelt

 14   Deer Flat National Wildlife Refuge: Nature Trail Habitat Hike

Best Hikes for Dogs

4   Hulls Gulch Interpretive Trail
15   Boise National Forest: Mores Mountain Interpretive Trail Extension
11   Reid W. Merrill Sr. Community Park: Eagle Pathways
16   Boise National Forest: Crooked River Trail

Best Hikes for Great Views

1   Oregon Trail Historic Reserve Trail System
3   Table Rock to Old Idaho State Penitentiary Trails
4   Hulls Gulch Interpretive Trail
15   Boise National Forest: Mores Mountain Interpretive Trail Extension
7   Polecat Gulch Reserve: Polecat Loop Trail
17   Bruneau Dunes State Park: Big Dune Hike

Best Hikes for Geology Lovers

3   Table Rock to Old Idaho State Penitentiary Trails
4   Hulls Gulch Interpretive Trail
17   Bruneau Dunes State Park: Big Dune Hike

Best Hikes for Nature Lovers

2   Boise River Greenbelt: Bethine Church River Trail
4   Hulls Gulch Interpretive Trail
15   Boise National Forest: Mores Mountain Interpretive Trail Extension
9   Garden City Greenbelt Pathway: River Pointe Park Nature Trail
14   Deer Flat National Wildlife Refuge: Nature Trail Habitat Hike

Best Hikes for History Buffs
   1   Oregon Trail Historic Reserve Trail System

   3   Table Rock to Old Idaho State Penitentiary Trails

Best Hikes for Pedestrians Only
   2   Boise River Greenbelt: Bethine Church River Trail

   4   Hulls Gulch Interpretive Trail

 15   Boise National Forest: Mores Mountain Interpretive Trail Extension

 10   Garden City Greenbelt Pathway: Riverside Pedestrian Path

1 Oregon Trail Historic Reserve Trail System

A combination of vast views of the lush river valley, basalt cliffs, and history make this trail a must-do. Learn about the Oregon Trail while hiking near intact ruts left by the original wagon trains. Both the Kelton Ramp and this section of the Oregon Trail in the reserve are listed on the National Register of Historic Places.

Distance: 2.7-mile loop with additional trail option

Approximate hiking time: 2 hours

Difficulty: Moderate; steep inclines to and from the basalt cliffs

Trail surface: Gravel single- and doubletrack; rock-strewn single-track

Best season: Best in early spring and late autumn

Other trail users: Bicyclists

Canine compatibility: Leashed dogs permitted

Fees and permits: No fees or permits required

Schedule: Year-round

Maps: Ridge to Rivers Trail System map, available at outdoor retail stores throughout Boise or online at www.ridgetorivers.org

Trail contacts: Boise Parks and Recreation Department, 1104 Royal Blvd., Boise 83706; (208) 384-4240; www.cityofboise.org/parks; Ridge to Rivers Trail System: (208) 514-3756

Special considerations: Stay on the designated trails to protect the original Oregon Trail wagon ruts. Trail hazards include rattlesnakes, extreme heat, seasonal fire danger, high winds, and hazardous cliffs.

Finding the trailhead: Take I-84 to exit 57 (Gowen Road). Turn north onto ID 21 heading toward Idaho City. At the junction of ID 21 and Federal Way, reset your tripometer to 0 and continue north on ID

21. At 2 miles turn right onto East Forest Lake Drive. Drive past the Kelton trailhead, used by buses, at 2.3 miles. At 2.8 miles turn right into the Whitman trailhead at 5000 East Forest Lake Dr.; park in the lot. The trail starts at the north side of the lot. GPS: N43 33.06' / W116 07.41'

The Hike

Travel beside the famous main route of the Oregon Trail on the reserve's Oregon and Rim Trails. This site is part of the 2,170-mile-long Oregon National Historic Trail. View the original wagon train ruts on the protected area beside the hiking trails. Three overlooks on the edge of the basalt cliffs on the Rim Trail provide unobstructed views of the lush Boise River valley below, and informative trail signs describe the area's history.

During the 1840s through the 1860s, approximately 300,000 westbound emigrants traveled the Oregon Trail from Missouri toward Oregon. Many passed through Idaho. The trail was rugged, and one out of eight travelers died on the trail. In 1836 the first cart passed through the area, followed by many thousands more, helping to establish a broad track. The route became less used when the railroads came to the area in 1884.

Hike down the Kelton Ramp, a trail off the basalt cliffs used by freight wagons, stagecoach passengers, and emigrants to access the oasis below the cliffs. Stroll below the black columnar lava decorated with bright green and orange lichen. The trail was manually cut into the basalt rocks in the mid-1860s and was part of the route between Salt Lake City, Utah, and Idaho City used during the gold rush.

The loop hike described here covers the reserve's Oregon Trail, Basalt Trail, and the overlooks on the Rim Trail. Numerous residential access points join the trail.

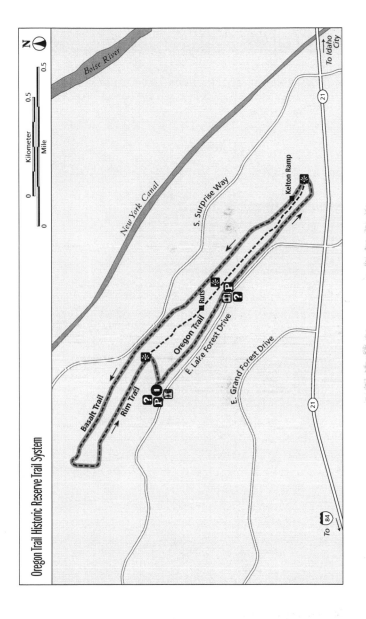

Oregon Trail Historic Reserve Trail System

Miles and Directions

0.0 Start on the doubletrack gravel trail at the north side of the parking lot by veering right (east). Travel 133 feet and turn right at the Y intersection, continuing east onto the Oregon Trail (trail number 103). (**Option:** Turn left to access the Whitman Overlook on the Rim Trail [102]).

0.4 Arrive at a trail junction. Continue on the Oregon Trail, heading east. (**Option:** Turn left for the Suhuwoki Overlook on the Rim Trail.)

0.5 The Kelton trailhead enters here. (FYI: Restrooms are available.) Continue east on the Oregon Trail. Look closely to the left (north). The original Oregon Trail wagon ruts are visible next to the hiking trail.

0.8 Veer left (north) on the doubletrack gravel trail, continuing on the Oregon Trail.

0.9 Arrive at the junction of Oregon, Rim, and Basalt (101) Trails. Visit the Kelton Overlook at this junction. Continue the loop by descending the Kelton Ramp, heading west off the basalt cliffs. The trail is steep and rock strewn.

1.1 Arrive at junction with the Basalt Trail. Turn left (west) onto the Basalt Trail, traveling between the cliffs to the south and residential homes to the north.

2.1 Near the large water tank by a dirt access road, turn left (south) and head up the trail as it ascends to the rim of the basalt rocks.

2.2 Arrive at the rim and turn left (east) at the Y junction onto the Rim Trail. Pass under power lines as the trail travels along the rim of the basalt cliffs.

2.6 Stop and enjoy the view from the Whitman Overlook just before the Y junction. At the junction turn right (uphill) to return to the parking lot. (**Option:** Stay left and complete the 0.9-mile stretch of the Rim Trail to the Kelton Ramp.)

2.7 Arrive the trailhead parking lot, having completed the loop. (**Option:** Hike the Rim Trail.)

2 Boise River Greenbelt: Bethine Church River Trail

Wildlife thrives in this twenty-four-acre natural area located next to the Boise River just minutes from busy downtown Boise. The wetlands and woods surrounding the trail provide food, shelter, water, and safe nesting areas wildlife need. Several canals in the area form a stream inhabited by fish.

Distance: 2.8-mile out-and-back
Approximate hiking time: 1 hour
Difficulty: Easy; level surface
Trail surface: Dirt, gravel, and grass
Best season: Spring through autumn
Other trail users: Pedestrians only
Canine compatibility: Leashed dogs permitted
Fees and permits: No fees or permits required
Schedule: Year-round
Maps: *DeLorme: Idaho Atlas & Gazetteer:* Page C4; DeLorme Topo USA 7.0; Ridge to Rivers Trail Map, available at outdoor retail shops throughout Boise or online at www.ridgetorivers.org. Boise River Greenbelt maps are available from the Boise Parks and Recreation Department.
Trail contacts: Boise Parks and Recreation Department, 1104 Royal Blvd., Boise 83706; (208) 384-4240; www.cityofboise.org/parks
Special considerations: Contact the Boise Parks and Recreation Department for updated information regarding future trailhead access on the eastern terminus. Fishing is allowed on the Boise River but not in the Protected Trout Habitat area.

Finding the trailhead: From I-84 take exit 54 (Broadway Avenue) and head north on US 20/26, which becomes Broadway Avenue. Drive about 2.2 miles and turn right (east) onto Beacon Street. At

2.5 miles cumulative, turn right onto West Park Center Boulevard, which soon becomes East Park Center Boulevard. Drive to East River Run Drive at 4.4 miles and turn left, then immediately right into Baggley Park. Park at the north end of the parking lot. GPS: N43 34.98' / W116 09.94'

The Hike

The trail segment described here starts at Baggley Park, connects with the Bethine Church River Trail, and then heads west, offering a taste of the pedestrian-only trail. This segment passes through a protected wildlife study area.

Named for Bethine Church, widow of former U.S. Senator Frank Church, this trail honors the natural world. The Church family was influential in protecting large tracks of Idaho wilderness through conservation efforts and public land policy, including the Frank Church River of No Return Wilderness, located in central Idaho.

Nestled along the south shore of the Boise River, the 1.6-mile Bethine Church River Trail preserves the wetland environment while permitting hiker access. It is part of the Boise River Greenbelt.

Intermittent benches encourage resting and contemplation. It is hard to imagine that the Boise River was severely polluted prior to the 1960s. Currently the now-clean river serves as a life-giving artery for the natural ecosystem and for the inhabitants of the Treasure Valley.

Check out the interpretive signs along the trail describing the belted kingfishers, Lewis's woodpeckers, and violet-green swallows you might see. Contributed by the WREN Foundation, the signs are part of the Idaho Birding Trail, a system of birding opportunities scattered across the state.

Miles and Directions

0.0 Start on the narrow paved trail on the north edge of the parking lot. The trail winds along the edge of the park near residences. View Table Rock in the distance to the north.

0.2 Turn left and walk about 20 feet through the short paved section between houses marked FIRE LANE, then turn right onto another, smaller paved path. After another 50 feet turn left onto South Swallowtail Lane, a residential road. Walk past ten homes.

0.3 Turn left at the trailhead signs indicating the Greenbelt Wildlife Reserve access onto a dirt/gravel trail. From this point on, the trail is for pedestrians only. (FYI: There is a bike rack for bicyclists.) The trail progresses between homes. Cross a footbridge over Logger Creek.

0.4 The trail comes to an intersection with the main doubletrack trail along the Boise River. The description here covers about a mile of the western segment of the 1.6-mile Bethine Church River Trail by heading downstream (west). (**Option:** Turn right [east], traveling about 0.5 mile of the eastern upstream trail segment that ultimately connects with Barber Park.) A Boise River Greenbelt mile marker comes into view ahead as the trail heads west. (FYI: The mileage shown on the marker is based on the total City of Boise Greenbelt system mileage and differs from this hike description.)

0.5 Cross another footbridge. Note the large, stately home to the south. The north side of the Boise River is readily visible.

0.8 The whitewater rapid observed on this section of the Boise River is commonly referred to as The Weir. Watch kayakers surfing on the wave created by water flowing over this decommissioned weir along Warm Springs Avenue, near the west edge of the Warm Springs Golf Course.

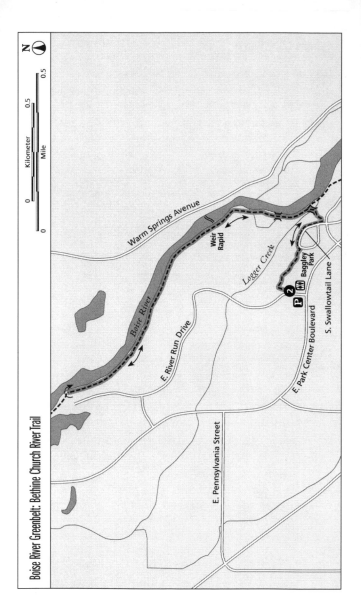

Boise River Greenbelt: Bethine Church River Trail

N

Kilometer
0   0.5

Mile
0   0.5

Boise River

Warm Springs Avenue

Weir Rapid

Logger Creek

E. River Run Drive

E. Pennsylvania Street

E. Park Center Boulevard

S. Swallowtail Lane

Baggley Park

P

2

1.0 Follow the trail past the Protected Trout Habitat, which is on the south side of the trail. Walk on a spit of land between an irrigation canal and the Boise River.

1.4 Arrive at the intersection with the paved portion of the Boise River Greenbelt. Retrace the route back to Baggley Park. (**Option:** Continue west on the paved greenbelt system, heading downstream.)

2.8 Arrive back at the trailhead.

3 Table Rock to Old Idaho State Penitentiary Trails

An uphill climb, starting from behind the Old Idaho State Penitentiary, traverses to the top of Table Rock's sandstone cliffs for a sweeping view of the Treasure Valley. Trailside interpretive signs describe the impact of various geological events on the vistas.

Distance: 3.3-mile lollipop
Approximate hiking time: 2 hours
Difficulty: Moderate; uneven rocky terrain and elevation gain on last portion of the trail
Trail surface: Singletrack trail and doubletrack road comprising a mix of rocks, dirt, and gravel
Best season: Spring and autumn
Other trail users: Mountain bikers, equestrians on lower trails, motorized vehicles on the top of Table Rock
Canine compatibility: Leashed dogs permitted in parking area; dogs under voice control permitted on the trail
Fees and permits: No fees or permits required
Schedule: Open year-round
Maps: USGS Boise South, Idaho–Ada County; *DeLorme:*

Idaho Atlas & Gazetteer: Page 35 C4; Ridge to Rivers Trail Map, available at outdoor shops throughout Boise or online at www.ridgetorivers.org
Trail contacts: City of Boise Parks and Recreation Department, 1104 Royal Blvd., Boise 83706; (208) 384-4240; www.cityofboise.org/parks; Ridge to Rivers Trail System: (208) 514-3756; Old Idaho State Penitentiary, 2445 Old Penitentiary Rd., Boise 83712; (208) 334-2844; www.idahohistory.net
Special considerations: Be cautious when walking near the cliff edge, and keep track of the kids. If mud sticks to your feet at or near the trailhead, protect the trails from further damage by hiking elsewhere.

Finding the trailhead: From I-84, take exit 54 (Broadway). Go north on US 20/26, locally called Broadway Avenue, for 3.1 miles to the intersection of Broadway Avenue, Idaho Street, Avenue B, and Warm Springs Avenue. Reset the tripometer to 0, and turn right (east) onto East Warm Springs Avenue. Travel 1.4 miles and turn left onto North Penitentiary Road. Proceed another 0.2 mile and turn left into the Old Idaho State Penitentiary parking lot, where Old Pen tours start. Continue 0.1 mile to the Old Penitentiary trailhead. Begin the hike at the northeast end of the large parking area. GPS: N43 36.22' / W116 09.75'

The Hike

This well-used trail combines history and geology, rewarding hikers with one of the best locations for viewing the valley. Table Rock is a Boise icon and a favorite site for entertaining visitors.

Start the hike in the busy trailhead parking lot behind the Bishop's House. Other trails in the area join the following route. Traverse upwards, passing near homes and along singletrack and doubletrack trails. Interpretive signs at a vista point describe the geological basis of the area.

The Boise River watershed provides vital life-giving water to the valley, in stark contrast to the desert outlined in the distance and the desert environment of the hike. Past volcanic action, the present underground geothermal systems, and the colorful sandstone cliff plateau afford a graphic geology lesson.

Atop the plateau, hikers, rock climbers, and motorized-vehicle users survey the 360-degree view. Tread carefully near the short cliffs while viewing the desert to the south and the Boise National Forest to the north.

Table Rock to Old Idaho State Penitentiary Trails

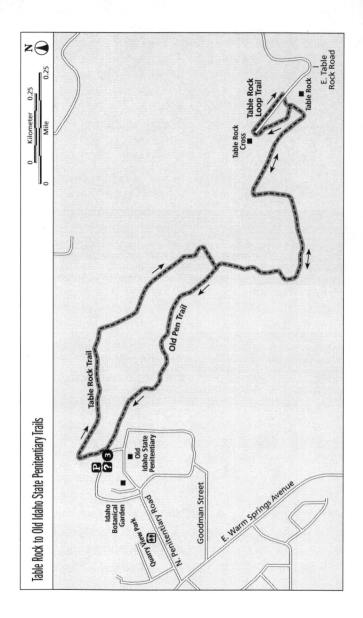

N

Kilometer 0.25

0

Mile 0.25

0

Table Rock Loop Trail

Table Rock Cross

Table Rock

E. Table Rock Road

Table Rock Trail

Old Pen Trail

Idaho Botanical Garden

Quarry View Park

N. Penitentiary Road

Old Idaho State Penitentiary

Goodman Street

E. Warm Springs Avenue

P

2 3

Table Rock isn't the only local icon. So is the tall cross, visible from many points in the valley both day and night. The capital city's tall buildings, the Boise airport, and residential homes spread out below the cliffs. End this hike by passing near the Old Idaho State Penitentiary, with its many sandstone buildings made of stone quarried from the surrounding cliffs.

Create a full day's adventure by adding a guided tour through the Old Idaho State Penitentiary or visiting the Idaho Museum of Mining and Geology, the Idaho Botanical Garden, and the nearby Quarry View Park picnic area.

NOTE: The first few hundred yards of the hike lead you away from your visual target, Table Rock.

Miles and Directions

0.0 Start the hike at the trailhead (2,778 feet elevation). Go about 85 feet, passing the Old Pen Trail (15A), and turn left. Travel another 35 feet, turning left at the junction of the Table Rock Trail (15) and Castle Rock Loop (19). At 263 feet from the trailhead, turn right at the junction with Castle Rock Loop onto Table Rock Trail. After climbing a steep, rocky trail portion, turn right (east) and continue on Table Rock Trail. The destination is now in view. The trail switchbacks, passing through vegetation and along lava rock, then levels out. Continue past unmarked feeder footpaths.

0.4 At junction of Table Rock Trail and Castle Rock Quarry Trail (18), continue right (east) on Table Rock Trail. The trail winds through a valley with large homes on the left. Table Rock looms ahead.

0.8 At junction of Old Pen and Table Rock Trails, turn left, continuing on the Table Rock Trail. (FYI: On your return you will take the Old Pen Trail.) Take a deep, full breath in preparation for the final ascent to Table Rock—and the steepest part of the hike—on a doubletrack dirt road.

1.1 Arrive at another junction. Continue straight ahead toward the top of Table Rock.

1.2 Turn left (west) onto Table Rock Trail. The route becomes steeper.

1.3 Take a breather—you're at 3,466 feet elevation—and read the interpretive signs describing the geological events that formed the valley below.

1.6 The trail arrives at the plateau, the top of Table Rock. There are multiple trails in the area. Continue hiking to the left and onto Table Rock Loop Trail (16), sharing the doubletrack trail with motorized vehicles. Look for the radio towers, turning left (south) in front of the towers. Continue to the large cross structure to the west.

1.8 Walk around the flat top of the sandstone rock, enjoying the 360-degree view. Return to Table Rock Trail, picking it up at the east corner of the radio tower where the trail emerged onto Table Rock.

2.0 Return down the hill via Table Rock Trail.

2.8 Arrive at the junction of Old Pen Trail and Table Rock Trail. Turn left onto the Old Pen Trail. Follow the singletrack trail down to a small drainage filled with willow trees and berry bushes. When the drainage opens, notice the Idaho Botanical Garden to the left and the Old Idaho State Penitentiary ahead.

3.3 Arrive back at the trailhead.

4 Hulls Gulch Interpretive Trail

Designated as a National Recreation Trail, the Hulls Gulch Interpretive Trail passes through two types of distinct habitats. Sagebrush grasslands are part of the Great Basin desert that lines the hillsides; maples, birches, and syringa grow along the creek bottom in the riparian zone. Rock outcroppings and a waterfall are but a few of the highlights on this trail. Interpretive signs provide information regarding the area's wildlife, geology, plants, and fire ecology.

Distance: 7.0-mile lollipop; 3.9-mile shuttle option

Approximate hiking time: 3 to 4 hours

Difficulty: Strenuous; uneven and steep terrain on the upper portion of the trail

Trail surface: Rocky, singletrack dirt path

Best season: May through October

Other trail users: Pedestrians only

Canine compatibility: Dogs under voice control permitted. Be ready to call and leash your pet.

Fees and permits: No fees or permits required

Schedule: Usually open year-round for hiking. A gate located about 0.2 mile from the lower

trailhead controls access for full-size and all-terrain vehicles (ATVs) to upper Eighth Street Road near the lower trailhead. The gate closes in December and typically reopens by mid-May. In late winter and early spring, when conditions are muddy, the trail may be closed to all uses, including hiking.

Maps: USGS Robie Creek; *DeLorme: Idaho Atlas & Gazetteer:* Page 35 C4; DeLorme Topo USA; Ridge to Rivers Trail Map, available at outdoor shops throughout Boise or online at www.ridgeto rivers.org

Trail contacts: Ridge to Rivers Trail System: (208) 514-3756; Bureau of Land Management: (208) 384-3300

Special considerations: Eighth Street Road closes during winter to protect the watershed and wildlife; access is controlled by a gate located 2.8 miles from the corner of State and North Eighth Streets.

April through July, sheep and cattle graze in the area. The sheep return to the area for grazing between October and December. Keep pets under control, especially during managed grazing months. Watch out for poison ivy, stinging nettles, and the occasional western rattlesnake.

Prepare for a self-sufficient trek. This hike is more remote than it first appears.

Finding the trailhead: From the intersection of State and North Eighth Streets, turn north onto North Eighth Street. Reset the tripometer to 0 and continue north on North Eighth Street. Enter the Hulls Gulch Reserve–Boise Recreation Front at 1.5 miles from State Street. The road becomes Sunset Peak Road (Eighth Street Road) and turns from paved to gravel. Continue another 0.5 mile, passing the Foothills Learning Center. The road then goes up a steep hill for 0.8 mile to the North Eighth Street Road gate. Continue another 0.2 mile past the open gate and turn right into the large parking lot at the lower trailhead. GPS N43 39.04' / W116 08.77'

Option: Proceed up the road to the smaller upper trailhead and drop a shuttle vehicle for a one-way point-to-point hike.

The Hike

The hike starts at 3,807 feet above the Snake River plain. Observe the effects of the 1996 Eighth Street fire on the upper Boise Front foothills and the resultant restoration efforts. Wide views of the distant valley, originally a large lake, are prevalent on the first part of the hike.

Continue downhill to the bottom of the drainage and enjoy the lush creek bottom. Given the sense of remoteness the trail offers, it is easy to imagine the residents of the drainage—coyotes, elk, and mule deer—keeping an eye on unsuspecting hikers from their perch on the steep hillsides.

Due to the vegetation and moistness of the creekbed, the riparian area is ripe for bird watching. Robins, orioles, yellow warblers, and finches flutter among chokecherries, elderberries, and arrowleaf balsamroot.

As the trail ascends the drainage, smooth granite rocks containing hues of pink and gray punctuate the hillsides. The upper reach of the gulch offers a loop approximately 1.0 mile in length. Though the terrain becomes rugged, it is well worth the effort. A rock outcropping, with a waterfall that runs in spring, stands as a backdrop for panoramic views of the valley below. It's an ideal spot for snacks and photographs.

Continue uphill to the small upper trailhead parking area beyond the wooden gate. Alternatively, complete the loop trail by heading southwest, returning to the main trail via a steep path that passes through a boulder field. Once back on the main trail, retrace your steps to complete the out-and-back hike.

Option: If you've planned for a point-to-point hike, pick up your shuttle vehicle at the upper trailhead.

Miles and Directions

0.0 Start at the southeast edge of the lower trailhead parking lot. Pass through the two sets of wooden trailhead gates. Note the interpretive information signs before turning right onto the lower trail. Head gradually downhill toward the creekbed and the trail intersection.

0.8 The trail intersects the Hulls Gulch Trail (29). Turn left (northeast) onto the Hulls Gulch Interpretive Trail (0). Continue upstream along the creekbed, crossing small bridges frequently and passing granite boulders.

Hulls Gulch Interpretive Trail

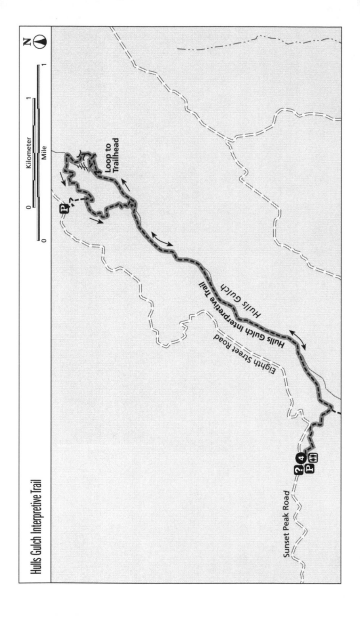

N

Kilometer

Mile

Loop to
Trailhead

P

Hulls Gulch Interpretive Trail

Hulls Gulch

Eighth Street Road

Sunset Peak Road

P

2.3 Continue to the junction marked by a wooden LOOP TO TRAILHEAD sign. Stay on the main trail by continuing straight ahead on the Hulls Gulch Interpretive Trail toward the upper trailhead. (**Option:** Turn left [north] and climb a steep switchback.) Either way, the best part of the hike lies ahead.

3.1 Arrive at a rock outcropping and a waterfall (seasonal) with a bridge. Enjoy the extensive views of the valley. More panoramic views lie ahead as you continue up the trail.

3.7 Turn left (north) at the next trail junction to get to the upper trailhead.

3.9 Arrive at the upper trailhead. (**Option:** If you've arranged for a shuttle, this is the end of your hike.) Alternatively, complete the loop by heading southwest on the less-used Loop Trail. The trail heads sharply downhill through boulder fields. Be careful of the loose stones on the trail.

4.7 Complete the loop, arriving back at the junction with the Hulls Gulch Interpretive Trail. Turn right onto the interpretive trail and retrace your route back to the lower trailhead.

7.0 Arrive back at the trailhead.

5 Veterans Memorial Park: Boise Cascade Lake Loop

For a refreshing hike on a hot summer afternoon, try this short hike near downtown Boise. The major portion of the trail travels beside various bodies of water, offering fishing, wildlife viewing, and swimming opportunities.

Distance: 1.3-mile loop

Approximate hiking time: 1 hour

Difficulty: Easy; flat terrain and paved portion

Trail surface: Dirt, gravel single- and doubletrack, and pavement

Best season: Spring through autumn

Other trail users: Bicyclists and in-line skaters

Canine compatibility: Dogs permitted on leash no longer than 8 feet

Fees and permits: No fees or permits required

Schedule: Year-round

Maps: *DeLorme: Idaho Atlas & Gazetteer:* Page 35 C4; DeLorme Topo USA 7.0; Ridge to Rivers Trail Map, available at outdoor shops throughout Boise or online at www.ridgetorivers.org; The Boise River Greenbelt, available from the City of Boise Parks and Recreation Department

Trail contacts: City of Boise Parks and Recreation Department, 1104 Royal Blvd., Boise 83706; (208) 384-4240; trail updates available at www.cityofboise.org

Special considerations: Watch out for poison ivy. Disturbing wildlife or collecting vegetation and natural objects is prohibited. Uniformed volunteers and Boise City police patrol the Greenbelt regularly, assisting users and reinforcing rules. Part-time rangers help bike officers during summer.

Finding the trailhead: Head west on State Street from the capitol building. At the intersection of State Street, 36th Street, and Veterans Way Boulevard, reset the tripometer to 0 and turn left (south)

onto Veterans Way Boulevard. Travel 0.2 mile and turn left (east) onto Stilson Road. Veer right, passing the entrance to Veterans Memorial Park on the left. Turn left into the paved trailhead parking lot beyond the park's entrance. Start the hike on the south end of the parking lot. GPS: N43 38.22' / W116 14.35'

The Hike

For water lovers, this trail is a real treat. Travel between the Boise Cascade Lake shoreline and the banks of canals and the Boise River. The hike starts in Veterans Memorial Park and connects with a portion of the 22.5-mile Boise River Greenbelt.

Currently the 200-acre park is maintained by the City of Boise. In 1997 the city acquired the park as a twenty-five-year lease from the state of Idaho. The grounds were once the site of the Soldiers Home, opened in 1895. Two fires and rebuilds later, the home closed in 1966. In 1976 the grounds emerged as Veterans Memorial State Park. Also in 1976, the Boise Cascade Corporation, headquartered in Boise, donated the lake and adjacent land to celebrate the bicentennial of the United States of America.

The north side of the lake is populated with shady trees and active wildlife, including squirrels and riparian zone birds. Hatchery-raised rainbow trout splash in the cool green waters of the lake, stocked regularly by the Idaho Fish and Game Department.

Arrive at the southern side of the lake by the wheelchair-accessible fishing dock; the gravel trail hooks onto the Boise River Greenbelt. This loop hike continues downstream along the Boise River on the paved trail beside the lake, with easy access to fishing and numerous wooden logs serving as rest benches.

There is a change of pace on the Boise River Greenbelt. In-line skaters, bicycle commuters, runners, leashed dogs, and families with baby strollers require alertness and proper Greenbelt etiquette. Stay to the right side of the pavement, and verbally notify those you are passing with a friendly greeting.

Continue walking along the lake. In the future the Ray Neef M.D. River Recreation Park, a whitewater park, will be adjacent to this trail. Kayakers and other paddle-powered boaters playing on the Boise River will add to the entertainment value of the hike.

The loop hike continues with a right turn off the paved Greenbelt near the lake's outlet, guiding hikers back into the cooler, calmer section of the trail. The trail returns to the bridge over the canal near the start point of the hike and the path to the trailhead.

Options: Return to the Boise River Greenbelt and extend the hike to the east or west. Or hang out at Veterans Memorial Park, enjoying the stately trees and a picnic.

Miles and Directions

0.0 Start on the paved doubletrack trail leading off the edge of the parking lot. Travel about 326 feet to the intersection with another paved path. Turn right onto the paved path and cross the bridge over the canal. After the bridge turn left (east) onto the doubletrack gravel trail that leads through the woods to the lake.

0.2 The lake comes into view at a bridge. Cross the bridge and turn left (east) to circumnavigate the jetty of land between the north shore of Boise Cascade Lake and the irrigation canal.

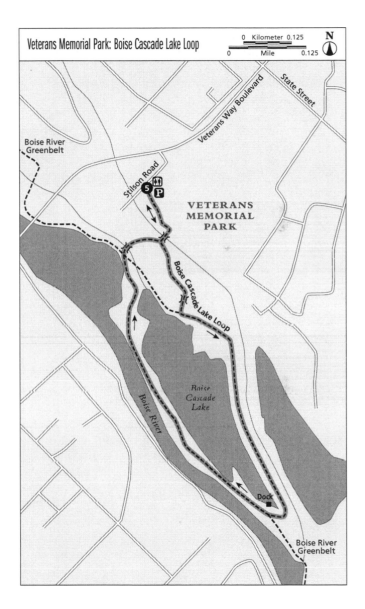

Veterans Memorial Park: Boise Cascade Lake Loop

0   Kilometer 0.125

0   Mile   0.125

N

Boise River
Greenbelt

Veterans Way Boulevard

State Street

Stilson Road

5

VETERANS
MEMORIAL
PARK

Boise Cascade Lake Loop

Boise River

Boise
Cascade
Lake

Dock

Boise River
Greenbelt

0.6 The lake tapers at the inflow at the eastern edge. Veer right onto a singletrack dirt trail leading to the paved Boise River Greenbelt, passing the fishing dock on the right.

0.7 Turn right (west) onto the paved trail and continue on the spit of land between the south shore of the lake and the bank of the Boise River. Head downstream on the Boise River Greenbelt. (**Option:** For a longer hike, turn left (east) and head upstream toward downtown Boise.)

1.1 Turn right off the Boise River Greenbelt onto another paved trail, crossing a bridge over the outlet of Boise Cascade Lake. Veer right after the bridge and continue on the paved trail. (**Option:** Remain on the Boise River Greenbelt, heading west downstream and ultimately connecting with the Garden City Greenbelt Pathway.)

1.2 Arrive at the junction of the start of the lake loop trail where the paved trail intersects the dirt trail. Return to the trailhead by staying left on the trail, crossing the canal bridge, and then turning left again to the parking lot.

1.3 Arrive back at the trailhead.

6 Corrals Trail: Miller Gulch Trailhead to Corrals–Bogus Basin Road Trailhead

Vast views of the Treasure Valley to the south and the Boise National Forest to the north characterize this short hike through open rangeland in the Boise Front Recreation Area.

Distance: 2.8-mile out-and-back
Approximate hiking time: 1 hour
Difficulty: Moderate; elevation gain at start of the hike
Trail surface: Singletrack; doubletrack sand, dirt, and gravel
Best season: Spring through autumn
Other trail users: Mountain bikers and equestrians
Canine compatibility: Dogs under voice control at all times permitted
Fees and permits: No fees or permits required
Schedule: Year-round
Maps: *DeLorme: Idaho Atlas & Gazetteer:* Page 35 C4; DeLorme Topo USA 7.0; Ridge to Rivers Trail Map, available at outdoor retail shops throughout Boise or online at www.ridgetorivers.org
Trail contacts: Ridge to Rivers Trail System: (208) 514-3756; Bureau of Land Management: (208) 384-3300
Special considerations: Cattle and sheep graze in the area, and wildlife makes a home here. Keep pets on-leash in the presence of domestic animals, and control pets at all times to minimize disturbing wildlife. If using other trails in the Corrals area, close all gates after you pass through. **NOTE:** Temporary trail closures occur when ground moisture is excessive and damage would occur due to trail use, typically during late winter and early spring.

Finding the trailhead: From I-84 take exit 53 and head north on Vista Avenue. Go 2.1 miles to the intersection with Capitol Boulevard

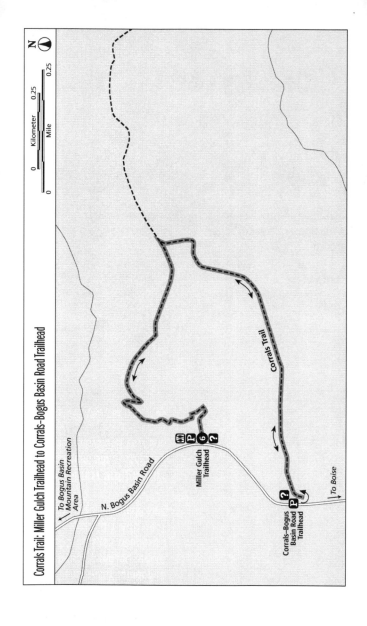

Corrals Trail: Miller Gulch Trailhead to Corrals–Bogus Basin Road Trailhead

To Bogus Basin Mountain Recreation Area

N. Bogus Basin Road

Miller Gulch Trailhead

Corrals Trail

Corrals–Bogus Basin Road Trailhead

To Boise

N

0   0.25
Kilometer
0   0.25
Mile

and veer left onto Capitol Boulevard. Continue north on Capitol Boulevard to 3.1 cumulative miles and turn left (west) onto West Front Street. Stay in the right lane and at 3.5 miles take the Front Street exit. At 3.7 miles turn right (north) at the stop sign onto 15th Street. Continue on 15th Street to 5.2 miles, arriving at the intersection with Hill Road. Turn left onto Hill Road and proceed to the intersection with Harrison Boulevard and North Bogus Basin Road (5.4 miles from I-84). Reset the tripometer to 0. Turn right (north) onto North Bogus Basin Road and travel 3.1 miles. Turn right into the Miller Gulch trailhead. GPS: N43 40.40' / W116 10.79'

Option: For a one-way hike, leave a car at the Corrals–Bogus Basin Road trailhead, located 2.8 miles from the intersection of North Hill Road and Harrison Boulevard. GPS: N43 40.49' / W116 10.33'

The Hike

This short hike provides a sample of the various trails in this area of the Ridge to Rivers Trail System.

The Corrals Trail is shared with ranchers with grazing rights. This part of the trail system passes through a mixture of public and private land. During spring, summer, and autumn, wildflowers bloom along the trail among the bitterbrush and sagebrush. Springtime brings out the pink filaree creeper. In summer look for the yellow arrowleaf balsamroot, a member of the sunflower family.

The steepest part of the hike is directly off the Miller Gulch trailhead parking area. Traverse the hillside, moving from 3,281 feet elevation to the plateau at 3,599 feet. Arriving at the saddle, the scenery opens up to include the Treasure Valley, with the Owyhee Mountains to the south, and the high peak of Shafer Butte in the Boise National Forest to the north.

The remainder of the hike along the ridge encompasses broad views of the Boise Front and the capital city below. Continue on the trail to the less-used Corrals–Bogus Basin Road trailhead.

Option: For a longer hike, return the way you came.

Miles and Directions

- **0.0**   Start at northeast section of the Miller Gulch trailhead parking lot, to the left of the vaulted toilet. Traverse up the hill, moving left.
- **0.5**   Arrive on the bench of a saddle where the 360-degree view opens up. The trail levels out and moves slightly up hill.
- **0.7**   At the junction with a doubletrack trail, indicated by a metal post marked CORRALS TRAIL (31), turn right (south) onto the doubletrack trail. Follow the ridge—at 3,600 feet elevation, the highest point of the hike.
- **1.2**   Travel down a gentle incline toward the roadside parking for another, undeveloped trailhead. The Miller Gulch trailhead is to the right, in the valley.
- **1.4**   Arrive at the kiosk and gate of the Corrals–Bogus Basin Road trailhead. (**Option:** If you left a car at this trailhead, your hike is over.) Turn around and return the way you came. (**Option:** Extend your hike on some of the other trails branching off the route described here.)
- **2.8**   Arrive back at the Miller Gulch trailhead.

7 Polecat Gulch Reserve: Polecat Loop Trail

Gently traverse sagebrush-covered hillsides and walk on high ridges offering views of Boise National Forest and the Treasure Valley below. Although near Boise, this hike provides a feeling of remoteness.

Distance: 6.2-mile loop

Approximate hiking time: 3 hours

Difficulty: More challenging; occasional steady uphill traverses and longer trail length

Trail surface: Sand, dirt single-track

Best season: Spring through autumn

Other trail users: Bicyclists and equestrians

Canine compatibility: Leashed dogs permitted; must be on a leash no longer than 6 feet at all times

Fees and permits: No fees or permits required

Schedule: Year-round

Maps: *DeLorme: Idaho Atlas & Gazetteer:* Page 35 C4; DeLorme Topo USA 7.0; Ridge to Rivers Trail Map, available at outdoor retail shops throughout Boise or online at www.ridgetorivers.org

Trail contacts: Ridge to Rivers Trail System: (208) 514-3756

Special considerations: Close the entry gate after you pass through it. Stay off the trail if it is muddy. Smoking is not permitted due to fire hazards. Hikers may experience cool and windy conditions on the ridges, so bring a jacket. Summers are hot and dry. Carry plenty of water and use sunscreen.

Finding the trailhead: From the capitol building in downtown Boise, head west on State Street to the intersection of Pierce Park Lane and West State Street. Reset the tripometer to 0 and turn right (north) onto North Pierce Park Lane. Cross over Hill Road at

1.1 miles and continue on North Pierce Park Lane (becoming North Pierce Park Road). At 3.8 miles cumulative, veer right at the Y intersection of North Pierce Park Road and North Cartwright Road onto North Cartwright Road. Go to 4.2 miles and turn right into the large gravel parking lot at the Polecat Gulch Reserve to access the Cartwright trailhead. GPS: N43 41.38' / W116 13.20'

The Hike

This loop trail features long, narrow ridges with grand views of the valleys and surrounding mountains. You can shorten this lengthy hike by using one of the two trails bisecting the loop. The trail system passes through public and private property and through a conservation easement. Private landowners donated property to the Ada County Soil and Water Conservation District, protecting the natural habitat and permanently preserving the land in the designated conservation easement against future development.

Halfway through the hike, the trail enters a valley. The old ranch house and dwellings came with the property purchased with the city's Foothills Levy funds and are owned by the City of Boise. A trailhead is planned near the site.

Watch for wildlife, which is often sighted along the reserve's trails. Deer, California quail, hawks, coyotes, and rattlesnakes are but a few of the local inhabitants you may see or hear.

In the mornings and evenings, the scent of sagebrush lingers in the air. Bitterbrush bushes bloom in the spring, producing yellow flowers.

Along a few stretches, hikers walk through dense growths of sagebrush lining the trail. Arrowleaf balsamroot, a member of the sunflower family, grows on the open hillsides and displays yellow flowers spring through autumn. Black beetles, as large as a quarter, scuttle across the sandy trails in the coolness of summer mornings and late evenings.

Boise's downtown district, and the Treasure Valley can be viewed from the ridges, reminding hikers of the urban nature of the surrounding area. Yet this long trail has a remote feel to it.

Miles and Directions

0.0 Start at the southwest edge of the parking area (3,313 feet elevation). Enter the trail by opening and closing a gate about 88 feet from the parking area. Start up the draw, turning right after 407 feet at the junction with the Polecat Loop Trail (81). (**FYI:** The trail to the left is the back end of the Polecat Loop Trail.) Traverse up the hill, along ridges, and into gullies.

2.2 Arrive at the intersection with the Doe Ridge Trail (82). Turn right to continue on the Polecat Loop Trail. On this stretch, the trail leaves the northwest ridges and heads south, with views of the Owyhee Mountains on the far south side of the Treasure Valley. At 3,475 feet, this is one of the highest elevation points on the hike. (**Option:** To shorten the hike, turn left (west) onto Doe Ridge Trail for a 3.2-mile loop.)

2.6 The trail heads steeply downhill, traversing off the ridge toward an old ranch house in a valley.

3.4 Turn left at the trail marker to continue on the Polecat Loop Trail. (**FYI:** The trail to the right goes toward the ranch house.) Head uphill through the small valley.

3.9 At the trail junction with the Quick Draw Trail (83) continue to the right (northeast) on the Polecat Loop Trail. Get ready for the steepest part of the hike as the trail switchbacks up to another ridge. (**Option:** Shorten the hike by turning left (north) onto Quick Draw Trail, which connects to Doe Ridge Trail and then back to the Polecat Loop Trail for a 5.1-mile loop.)

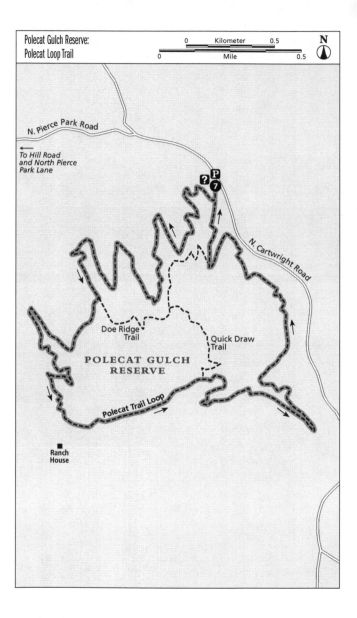

Polecat Gulch Reserve:
Polecat Loop Trail

0   Kilometer   0.5

0   Mile   0.5

N

N. Pierce Park Road

To Hill Road
and North Pierce
Park Lane

? P 7

N. Cartwright Road

Doe Ridge
Trail

Quick Draw
Trail

POLECAT GULCH
RESERVE

Polecat Trail Loop

Ranch
House

4.3 Arrive at on a ridge (3,416 elevation), with views of Shafer Butte in Boise National Forest to the north and the City of Boise to the south. Trails in the Owyhee Motorcycle Club Raceway are visible on the hillside across the valley.

4.6 The trail turns sharply left and travels along the contour line, paralleling North Cartwright Road, located below the hill. Several portions of the trail are covered in course sand, creating a challenge for bicyclers. Deer are often sighted along the trail in this area.

5.8 Pass the last trail junction where Doe Ridge Trail enters Polecat Loop Trail on the left. Continue to the right, heading down the trail toward the parking lot.

6.2 Arrive back at the trailhead.

8 Hidden Springs: Red Tail and Lookout Loop Trails

Located in a secluded valley near the community of Hidden Springs, this trail offers a quick, steep hike in the Dry Creek drainage. A short ascent opens to views of Boise National Forest and the growing residential development.

Distance: 1.1-mile lollipop
Approximate hiking time: 30 minutes
Difficulty: Moderate; significant elevation gain in a short distance
Trail surface: Dirt, sand single-track
Best season: Spring through autumn
Other trail users: Mountain bikers and equestrians
Canine compatibility: Dogs permitted under voice control and within 30 feet of owner.
Fees and permits: No fees or permits required

Schedule: Open year-round, except when soil is wet
Maps: *DeLorme: Idaho Atlas & Gazetteer:* Pages 34 C3 and 35 C3; DeLorme Topo USA 7.0; Ridge to Rivers Trail System map, available at outdoor shops throughout Boise or online at www.ridgetorivers.org
Trail contacts: Ridge to Rivers Trail System: (208) 514-3756
Special considerations: Trails in the area may shift as residential growth at Hidden Springs continues. Consult the Ridge to Rivers Web site for updates.

Finding the trailhead: From the capitol building in Boise, head west on State Street to the intersection of Gary Lane and Glenwood Street. Reset the tripometer to 0. Turn right (north) onto Gary Lane and go 1.1 miles to the intersection of Hill Road Parkway and Hill Road. Turn left onto Hill Road Parkway, veering right at 1.4 cumulative miles toward Hidden Springs onto North Seamans Gulch Road.

Continue to the intersection with Dry Creek Road at 5.7 miles. Turn right onto Dry Creek Road, which becomes West Dry Creek Road. At 6.8 miles turn right into the gravel parking lot that serves as the trailhead. The trail starts on the north side of the road. GPS: N43 43.52' / W116 14.82'

The Hike

After briefly paralleling the road, the trail switchbacks up the hillside and opens onto a saddle. The trail swings in a 360-degree turn around a knob, affording panoramic views of Hidden Springs to the south. A farmstead, built in the 1860s, sits in the woods along Dry Creek. One of the oldest intact farmhouses in Idaho, it is on the National Register of Historic Places.

From the north side of the knob, glance into the Current Creek drainage or gaze at pyramid-shaped Stack Rock in Boise National Forest. In spring, wildflowers bloom in all the colors of the rainbow and the cheatgrass glows a soft green. Sagebrush, bitterbrush, and rabbitbrush add other shades of green along the trail. During autumn, the trees in the community below blaze yellow, orange, and red. Coyotes, deer, foxes, and hawks reside in the open spaces around Hidden Springs, making wildlife sightings a real possibility during your hike.

Miles and Directions

0.0 Start the hike by heading east, crossing West Dry Creek Road and entering the Red Tail Trail (71) at the signpost (2,871 feet elevation).

0.4 At the first intersection near the saddle, go left onto the Lookout Loop Trail (72), the start of the traverse around the knob reaching an elevation of nearly 3,030 feet. On the

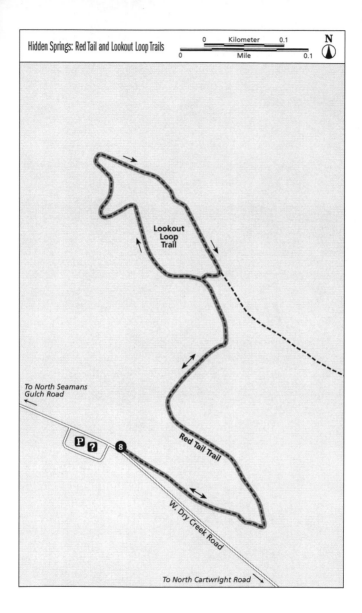

Hidden Springs: Red Tail and Lookout Loop Trails

0   Kilometer   0.1
0   Mile   0.1

N

Lookout Loop Trail

To North Seamans Gulch Road

P ? 8

Red Tail Trail

W. Dry Creek Road

To North Cartwright Road

north side of the loop, note the basalt outcroppings and Stack Rock in the distance.

0.7 Arrive at the saddle, continuing to the right to finish the loop. Reconnect with the Red Tail Trail in a few hundred feet. Start the descent back to the trailhead the way you came. (**Option:** Pick up trails off the saddle for further exploration.)

1.1 Arrive back at the trailhead.

9 Garden City Greenbelt Pathway: River Pointe Park Nature Trail

Enjoy a short hike on a nature trail just off the Garden City Greenbelt Pathway, followed by a stroll along the Boise River. Trailside interpretive signs describe the insects and wildlife inhabiting the wetland environment, setting the tone for exploring other parts of the Greenbelt.

Distance: 2.6-mile out-and-back
Approximate hiking time: 1-hour
Difficulty: Easy; flat terrain
Trail surface: Asphalt
Best season: Year-round
Other trail users: Bicyclists and in-line skaters
Canine compatibility: Leashed dogs permitted
Fees and permits: No fees or permits required
Schedule: Year-round
Maps: Parks and trails map, available from Garden City's City Hall or online at www.gardencity idaho.govoffice.com. View maps of adjacent trails at the City of Boise Web site (www.cityofboise .org), the City of Eagle Web site (www.cityofeagle.org), and the Ridge to Rivers Trail System Web site (www.ridgetorivers.org).
Trail contacts: City Hall (Garden City), 6015 Glenwood St., Garden City 83714; (208) 472-2900; www.gardencityidaho .govoffice.com
Special considerations: Watch out for poison ivy on the edges of the trail. Mosquitoes are common. During high-water season—late spring and early summer—the tunnel under Glenwood Street Bridge may be temporarily closed. Alternative trail access during high water is at the library parking lot on the west side of Glenwood Street.

Finding the trailhead: From the capitol building in downtown Boise, take State Street west toward Garden City. At the intersection of Gary Lane and Glenwood Street, reset the tripometer to 0 and turn left (south) onto Glenwood Street. Proceed 0.6 mile to Marigold Street and turn left (east) and then immediately left again into the large gravel parking lot on the southeast side of the Glenwood Street bridge. The hike starts from the northwest corner of the lot. GPS: N43 39.62' / W116 16.76'

The Hike

Start the hike at the streamflow-gaging station near the bridge and head downstream on the south side of the river on the Garden City Greenbelt Pathway. The trail immediately goes through a tunnel under the bridge. View the murals of whitewater rafters, a trout, and a bicyclist painted on the underpass wall. After leaving the tunnel, turn left off the main Greenbelt Pathway onto the River Pointe Park Nature Trail—a paved 0.3-mile side trail. Developed by the Rotary Club, this nature trail features interpretative signs describing the ecosystem found along the river. Picnic tables, convenient parking, proximity to restaurants, and the Garden City Library/City Hall make this segment of the Greenbelt a quick and interesting hike.

Trail users are likely to see majestic great blue herons, playful mallard ducks, and frisky rainbow trout on and in the river. Beaver, a nocturnal creature, and mink inhabit this area. Mature black cottonwood and silver maple trees provide constant shade along the route.

As you travel beside the sparkling river, contemplate the fact that the average family uses 240 gallons of water per day. The Boise River provides irrigators and citizens a reliable water source year-round.

After completing the nature trail, rejoin the Garden City Greenbelt Pathway and head west, passing apartment complexes, then expensive homes nestled next to the trail.

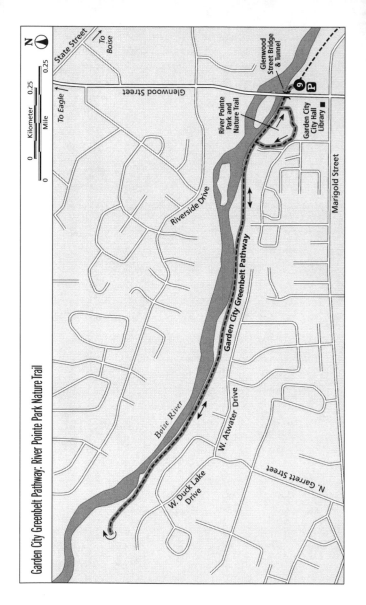

Garden City Greenbelt Pathway: River Pointe Park Nature Trail

N

0   0.25   Kilometer
0   0.25   Mile

State Street
To Boise
To Eagle
Glenwood Street
Glenwood Street Bridge & Tunnel
River Pointe Park and Nature Trail
Garden City City Hall Library
9
P
Boise River
Riverside Drive
Garden City Greenbelt Pathway
W. Atwater Drive
W. Duck Lake Drive
N. Garrett Street
Marigold Street

For a longer outing on the Greenbelt system, head east from the Glenwood Street bridge trailhead. The trail connects to the rest of the Garden City Greenbelt Pathway and ultimately to the City of Boise portion of the Boise River Greenbelt. The nearby On the River Campground serves as home base for out-of-towners exploring other Boise trails.

Miles and Directions

0.0 Start the hike by the Glenwood Street bridge and turn left (west) onto the paved portion of the Garden City Greenbelt Pathway. Pass through the tunnel under the bridge. About 364 feet from the start of the trail, turn left onto the River Pointe Park Nature Trail.

0.3 Rejoin the Garden City Greenbelt Pathway, proceeding west (downstream) along the Boise River.

1.3 The paved portion of the trail ends just after a small bridge. Turn around and retrace the Garden City Greenbelt Pathway to the trailhead.

2.6 Arrive back at the trailhead.

10 Garden City Greenbelt Pathway: Riverside Pedestrian Path

Enjoy a peaceful walk along the Boise River's north bank next to beautiful residential homes on this pedestrian–only trail. Mature cottonwoods and silver maples provide shade in summer and colorful foliage in autumn. Prolific birdlife adds harmonious songs to the rush of the river water.

Distance: 3.0-mile out-and-back

Approximate hiking time: 1 hour

Difficulty: Easy; level surface

Trail surface: Gravel, dirt doubletrack trail

Best season: Year-round

Other trail users: Pedestrians only

Canine compatibility: Leashed dogs permitted

Fees and permits: No fees or permits required

Schedule: Year-round

Maps: Parks and trails map, available from Garden City's City Hall or online www.gardencity idaho.govoffice.com. View maps of adjacent trails at the City of Boise Web site (www.cityofboise .org), the City of Eagle Web site (www.cityofeagle.org), and the Ridge to Rivers Trail System Web site (www.ridgetorivers.org).

Trail contacts: City Hall (Garden City), 6015 Glenwood St., Garden City 83714; (208) 472-2900; www.gardencityidaho .govoffice.com

Special considerations: During high water—late spring and early summer—portions of the trail may be wet. Watch out for poison ivy on the edges of the trail. Mosquitoes are common.

Finding the trailhead: From the capitol building in downtown Boise, take State Street west toward Garden City. At the intersection of Gary Lane and Glenwood Street, reset the tripometer to 0 and turn left (south) onto Glenwood Street. Proceed 0.3 mile to Riverside Drive and turn right (west). Continue to 0.4 mile and turn left into the small parking lot at Riverside Park, located on the north shore of the Boise River by Riverside Pond. The hike starts on the west side of the lot. GPS: N43 39.79' / W116 16.94'

The Hike

Designated for foot traffic only, this trail offers a peaceful, leisurely atmosphere. The trail starts at a stocked fishing pond, so if you have a license, you can add fishing to your outing. Casting a line into the Boise River is another option.

The tall trees above and the undercover below teem with birdlife. Yellow warblers, red-winged blackbirds, and mourning doves serenade walkers. Bald eagles nest in the area during winter. Great blue herons abide here year-round. Mergansers, mallards, and wood ducks bob along the river in spring.

Take a moment to look into a river eddy, a canal, or pond along the trail. Smaller creatures of the wetland ecosystem, such as water striders, flutter on the water, while dragonflies cruise through the air. Enjoy wild blackberries in late summer, and admire the cattails and wild roses in season. Note the metal chicken wire around the bottoms of some of the trees, protecting the tree trunks from the busy beavers prevalent along the river.

Miles and Directions

0.0   Start the trail at the west side of the parking area. After about 400 feet the trail moves away from the road and heads between the riverbank and residences.

0.4   Enter the Garden City Wildlife Habitat Area and the inlet of a small linear pond. The homes are set farther back from the trail at this point.

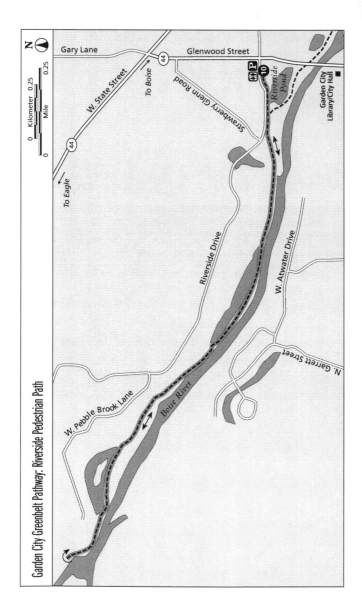

Garden City Greenbelt Pathway: Riverside Pedestrian Path

N

0   Kilometer 0.25
0   Mile   0.25

Gary Lane
Glenwood Street
44
To Boise
W. State Street
To Eagle
44
Strawberry Glenn Road
Riverside Pond
10
P
Garden City Library/City Hall
Riverside Drive
W. Atwater Drive
N. Garrett Street
Boise River
W. Pebble Brook Lane

0.7 Cross a wooden bridge at the outflow of a pond.

1.0 Walk on the spit of land between the river and a canal feeding the ponds. During low water levels, notice the noisy rapids in the river.

1.2 In the next stretch the trail moves briefly away from the river and near a canal, then back to the riverbank.

1.4 Overhead vegetation thins and the Boise River splits into North and South Channels.

1.5 The pedestrian trail ends at the gated homes at Ulmer Hollow. Retrace the trail back to the trailhead at Riverside Park. (**Option:** Continue through the Ulmer Street residential area and join the western Garden City Greenbelt Pathway, ultimately connecting with the Eagle Pathways.)

3.0 Return to the Riverside Park trailhead. (**Option:** To return to Glenwood Street, connect with the Garden City Greenbelt Pathway heading east and then the Boise River Greenbelt.)

11 Reid W. Merrill Sr. Community Park: Eagle Pathways

Located along the North Channel of the Boise River, the trail meanders alongside the waterway, which runs year-round. Stroll among ancient cottonwood trees, with glimpses of Boise National Forest to the north.

Distance: 1.4-mile out-and-back

Approximate hiking time: 30 minutes

Difficulty: Easy; flat surface

Trail surface: Asphalt paths, gravel, and dirt doubletrack

Best season: Year-round

Other trail users: Bicyclists, in-line skaters, equestrians

Canine compatibility: Leashed dogs permitted

Fees and permits: No fees or permits required

Schedule: Trailhead accessible dawn to dusk

Maps: *DeLorme: Idaho Atlas &*
Gazetteer: Page 34 C3; *Eagle Parks & Recreation Guide,* available from Eagle City Hall

Trail contacts: Eagle City Hall, 660 East Civic Lane, Eagle 83616; (208)939-6813; www .cityofeagle.org

Special considerations: Trail systems in the area are rapidly developing. Expect improvements in the future, including additional paved sections. The bridge underpass at Eagle Road may temporarily close during high water on the Boise River in spring and early summer.

Finding the trailhead: From the capitol building in downtown Boise, take West State Street toward Eagle. West State Street becomes ID 44 as you pass into Garden City on the way to Eagle. Continue on ID 44 to the stoplight at the intersection of Eagle Road and ID 44. Reset the tripometer to 0 and turn left (south) onto Eagle Road. Go 0.2 mile to the next stoplight and turn left onto Riverside Drive. Continue to 0.3 mile and turn right onto East Shore Drive.

Travel to 0.5 mile and turn right into Reid W. Merrill Sr. Community Park. The trailhead is located at the west end of the park. GPS: N43 41.28' / W116 20.84'

The Hike

For a taste of the trails in the Eagle Pathways system along the Boise River, try this shaded walk. The following description covers a hike west of the park trailhead along the north side of the North Channel of the Boise River, with options to continue west, east, or south on the trail system.

The majority of this hike moves along the river and past ponds. Enjoy bird watching and fishing along the way. Complete the brief out-and-back trek described below, or check out some of the hike extensions.

East of Reid W. Merrill Sr. Community Park a bridge crosses over the North Channel of the Boise River. It provides access to trails on the south side of the North Channel, including a pastoral walk along the river and near large homes.

Beyond the eastern portion of the route described here, the trail heads upstream (east). The gravel and dirt trail moves along the north side of the North Channel, through the woods, and past ponds. For an extension of the hike, continue to about 3.3 miles from the trailhead to where the trail passes through a residential area. This is a good turn-around point if you want to maintain the sense of being close to nature and away from development. Ultimately the eastbound trail connects with the Garden City Greenbelt Pathway and the Boise River Greenbelt through Boise.

Another option is to go downstream on the western paved portion of the trail near Reid W. Merrill Sr. Community Park. The trail passes under the Eagle Road bridge.

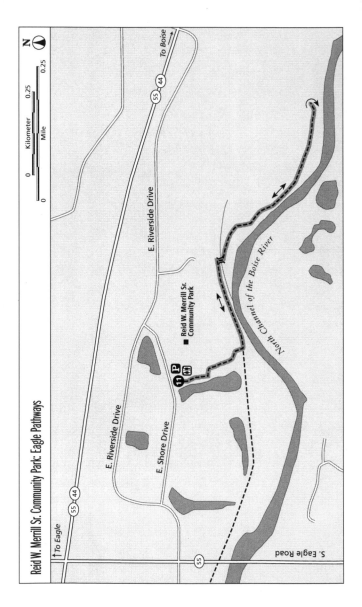

Reid W. Merrill Sr. Community Park: Eagle Pathways

To Eagle
55 44
To Boise
55 44

E. Riverside Drive
E. Riverside Drive
E. Shore Drive

Reid W. Merrill Sr. Community Park

11 P

North Channel of the Boise River

S. Eagle Road

N

0   0.25   Kilometer
0   0.25   Mile

Continue for 0.5 mile to a junction with another paved trail heading west beside ID 44 for about 1.5 miles to Ballantyne Road.

Miles and Directions

0.0 To get to this section of the Eagle Pathways system, walk the small paved trail at the west edge of the park.

0.1 Cross the footbridge over a dry canal and come to the junction with this paved segment of the Eagle Pathways system. Turn left (east) to follow the trail upstream. (**Option:** Turn right to follow the paved trail westward, passing under the Eagle Road bridge and near restaurants.)

0.2 Come to a bridge on the right (south) crossing over the North Channel of the Boise River; continue west on the main trail. (**Option:** Detour over the bridge for trails on the south side of the Boise River's North Channel.)

0.4 Arrive at a Y junction. Stay right, cross the footbridge, and veer left. (FYI: The left side of the Y leads to private property.)

0.7 Cross a footbridge and encounter a paved trail next to ponds in the River District development. This is your turn-around point. Return to the trailhead by retracing your route. (**Option:** Turn right (east) on the paved trail that becomes a dirt trail, continuing toward Garden City on the north side of the North Channel via the Eagle Pathways system.)

1.1 Return to the Y junction after crossing the footbridge. Stay to the left on the main trail and continue west.

1.2 Pass the bridge over the river.

1.3 Arrive at the intersection of this segment of the Eagle Pathways system and Reid W. Merrill Sr. Community Park. Turn right to return to the park and the trailhead. (**Option:** Continue west on the paved trail to the bridge underpass and restaurants.)

1.4 Arrive back at the trailhead.

12 Avimor: Burnt Car Draw Trail

Views of pyramid-shaped Stack Rock and the alpine slopes of Boise National Forest are constant companions on this hike through desert sagebrush, bunchgrass, and wildflowers. The remoteness of the upland rangeland reminds hikers that the Wild West—where the deer and elk roam—still exists.

Distance: 4.8-mile out-and-back

Approximate hiking time: 2 to 3 hours

Difficulty: More challenging; steep and continuous uphill climb

Trail surface: Dirt doubletrack

Best season: Year-round

Other trail users: Bicyclists and equestrians

Canine compatibility: Leashed dogs permitted at trailhead. Dogs must be on-leash from Oct 1 through May 31 for protection of big game during hunting season and nesting and migrating birds in the spring.

Fees and permits: No fees or permits required

Schedule: Burnt Car Draw and Spring Valley Creek trails are open year-round. Other trails close seasonally for wildlife protection, bird nesting and migration, and hunting season.

Maps: DeLorme Topo USA 7.0; trail map available at Avimor Sales Office or online at www .avimor.com

Trail contacts: Avimor Sale Office, 18454 North McLeod Way, Boise 83714; (208) 939-5360; www.avimor.com

Special considerations: Most of the trails are on private land. Use only the designated trails and avoid trespassing. Honor temporary and permanent trail closures. Hikers yield to equestrians and wildlife. Stay off the trails when they are muddy.

Finding the trailhead: Take ID 44 (West State Street) to the intersection with ID 55 North. Reset the tripometer to 0 and turn north onto ID 55. Travel 7.5 miles and turn right (east) onto West Avimor Drive at the entrance into the Avimor residential community. At 7.6 cumulative miles, turn right into the large trailhead parking lot. From the parking lot walk east about 0.2 mile on West Avimor Drive to the trailhead. GPS: N43 46.41' / W116 15.62'

The Hike

Though just off the highway, the Burnt Car Draw Trail quickly leads hikers away from the hustle of the road and into wide-open rangeland. The Boise National Forest looms on the horizon throughout the hike. Despite the long and challenging hike, the views of the undeveloped foothills, distant forest, and Treasure Valley far below are worth the effort.

Multiple landowners control the nearly 80 miles of trails in 35,000 acres of land in the SunCor Trust, which may ultimately connect with the Ridge to Rivers Trail System. The Bureau of Land Management, private ranchers, and the Avimor residential development collaborate for planned managed use of the land by various user groups and for habitat protection.

A 400-acre permanent conservation easement has been established, identified by the wildlife-friendly fencing. Only the middle strand of the fence's three horizontal strands contains barbs. The conservation easement, held by the Ada County Soil and Water Conservation District, permanently protects the habitat and restricts development of any kind in the designated area. Additionally, there are 550 acres of natural open space protected within the Avimor development boundary.

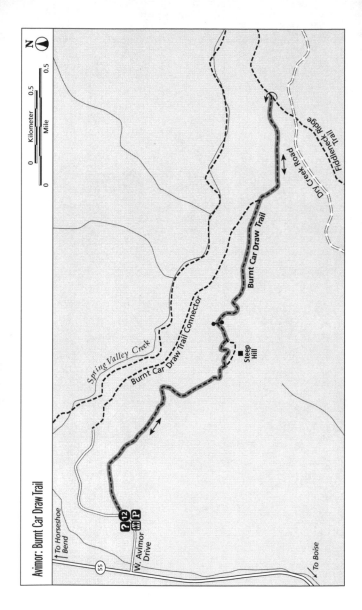

Avimor: Burnt Car Draw Trail

N

Kilometer
0   0.5
Mile
0   0.5

To Horseshoe Bend

55

W. Avimor Drive

To Boise

Spring Valley Creek

Burnt Car Draw Trail Connector

Burnt Car Draw Trail

Steep Hill

DTV Creek Road

Fiddleneck Ridge Trail

Elk winter in the area; 1,500 head were counted one winter. Deer are common, and bears and mountain lions are occasionally seen. Numerous migratory and residential birds inhabit the area. Wildflowers bloom from March through October. Yet the overriding asset of hiking in this area is the vastness of the landscape.

Miles and Directions

0.0 Start at the trailhead (3,237 feet elevation) at the end of West Avimor Drive, heading east on the Burnt Car Draw Trail (10). After 234 feet, a feeder path comes in on the left. Remain on the main trail, a doubletrack dirt road, and continue east along Burnt Car Draw. An intermittent creek runs through the draw on the far right.

1.1 The trail starts up an extremely steep hill. **Option:** Use the 0.2-mile singletrack trail. Rejoin the main trail at the top of the steep part of the hill.

1.2 Arrive at the saddle. Pass through a gate, closing it behind you. Continue up the gradual hills, with views of the Treasure Valley and the Owyhee Mountains to the south.

1.9 The trail encounters the first marked trail junction where Burnt Car Draw Connector Trail (10A) comes in on the left. Continue straight ahead (east) up a gradual hill on Burnt Car Draw Trail.

2.4 Arrive at the marked trail junction with Fiddleneck Ridge Trail (13) turning off to the right. This is your turnaround point (3,900 feet elevation). Walk a few hundred yards on Burnt Car Draw beyond the junction marker to enjoy a 360-degree view of Boise National Forest, Treasure Valley, and upland rangeland. It is downhill to the trailhead from here. (**Option:** Continue on the trail system for a longer hike.)

4.8 Arrive back at the trailhead on West Avimor Drive.

13 Kuna: Indian Creek Greenbelt

This short greenbelt offers variety. During the irrigation season, typically April through September, the creek along the trail glitters in the sunshine and expands activity options to include fishing, tubing, canoeing, and kayaking. After a jaunt on the trail, you can readily access a restaurant for a quick bite to eat.

Distance: 1.2-mile out-and-back

Approximate hiking time: 30 minutes

Difficulty: Easy; flat, smooth terrain

Trail surface: Paved (asphalt)

Best season: Spring through autumn

Other trail users: Bicyclists and in-line skaters

Canine compatibility: Leashed dogs permitted

Fees and permits: No fees or permits required

Schedule: Open dawn to dusk

Maps: *DeLorme: Idaho Atlas & Gazetteer:* Page 24 A3 and 34 C3; DeLorme Topo USA 7.0

Trail contacts: Kuna Chamber of Commerce, 123 Swan Falls Rd., Kuna 83634; (208) 922-9254; www.kunachamber.com

Finding the trailhead: From Boise take I-84 to exit 44 (Meridian/Kuna). At the end of the off-ramp, reset the tripometer and turn left (south) onto ID 69 (Western Heritage Historic Byway). Continue for about 7 miles, staying right when the road curves to the right and becomes North Kuna/Meridian Road. At 7.4 miles the road name changes to East Avalon Street. At 8.1 miles turn left onto South Swan Falls Road and then turn immediately right into the Kuna Chamber of Commerce Visitor Center. The hike starts at the Indian

Creek Greenbelt Park trailhead on the east end of the parking lot near the bridge over Indian Creek. GPS: N43 29.27' / W116 24.84'

The Hike

Kuna (pronounced *Q-nuh*) is a small rural town of approximately 14,000 residents. The town was originally a stagecoach stop on the route between Boise and mining towns in the Owyhee Mountains.

Head to the Indian Creek Greenbelt to admire the sparkling creek when it runs during irrigation season or to partake in other recreation activities available year-round. You can combine a hike with fishing, picnicking, and bird watching.

An active Union Pacific rail track is on the other side of the creek. There is a BMX bicycle park along the paved portion of the trail. Consider taking a trailside break to enjoy a pizza, steak, or salad at one of the restaurants in town or just off the trail.

The little town of Kuna is the gateway to the Snake River Birds of Prey National Conservation Area and the 30-mile Western Heritage Historic Byway. Pick up a scenic highway map, the raptor identification guide, and other brochures from the visitor center by the trailhead.

Miles and Directions

0.0 Start at the east end of the Indian Creek Greenbelt trailhead and head west on the wide, smooth asphalt.

0.2 Stay left at the Y junction to continue on the trail, passing the Kuna History Center. (FYI: Bearing right leads to the skateboard park.)

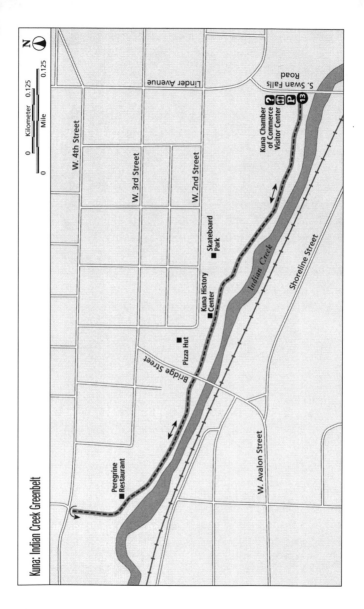

Kuna: Indian Creek Greenbelt

Peregrine Restaurant

Bridge Street

Pizza Hut

Kuna History Center

Skateboard Park

Indian Creek

W. Avalon Street

Shoreline Street

W. 2nd Street

W. 3rd Street

W. 4th Street

Linder Avenue

S. Swan Falls Road

Kuna Chamber of Commerce Visitor Center

13

N

0   Kilometer   0.125

0   Mile   0.125

0.4 At the next Y junction continue left under the West Avalon Street/Bridge Street bridge. Note the basalt rocks. (**Option:** Take a right at the Y to the Pizza Hut Restaurant.) After the bridge, pass the Indian Creek BMX Bike Park.

0.6 Arrive at the end of the paved section at West Fourth Street. Return the way you came. (**Option:** Stop to eat at the Peregrine Restaurant on the north side of the trail near the turnaround point.)

1.2 Arrive back at the trailhead.

14 Deer Flat National Wildlife Refuge: Nature Trail Habitat Hike

Located on the Pacific Flyway bird migratory path, the refuge on the shore of Lake Lowell near Nampa is a designated Watchable Wildlife site famous for its bird–watching opportunities. Views of the mountains in the Boise National Forest are to the north; the distant Owyhee Mountains are visible to the south. Grab a trail pamphlet from the visitor center for your own self-guided nature tour.

Distance: 0.6-mile loop

Approximate hiking time: 30 minutes

Difficulty: Easy; flat, gentle terrain

Trail surface: Gravel and dirt singletrack

Best season: Spring and autumn

Other trail users: Bicyclists

Canine compatibility: Leashed dogs permitted

Fees and permits: No fees or permits required

Schedule: Open daylight hours, year-round. Visitor center is open 8:00 a.m. to 4:00 p.m. Monday through Friday; 10:00 a.m. to 4:00 p.m. on Saturday; closed Sunday and federally recognized holidays.

Maps: *DeLorme Idaho Atlas & Gazetteer:* Page 24 A3 and 34 C3; DeLorme Topo USA 7.0; trail map available at the visitor center and trailhead

Trail contacts: Deer Flat National Wildlife Refuge, 13751 Upper Embankment Rd., Nampa 83686; (208) 467-9278; www .fws.gov/deerflat

Special considerations: The entrance gates to the visitor center, located at the intersection of Upper Embankment Road and Roosevelt Avenue, close at 4:00 p.m. between October 1 and April 14, at dusk the rest of the year. Refuge visitation is allowed during daylight hours only.

Stay on the designated trail. Areas off the Nature Trail are closed to minimize environmental impact.

Finding the trailhead: Take I-84 west from Boise to exit 33A. At the end of the ramp, reset the tripometer to 0 and turn left (west) onto ID 55 heading toward Marsing. The highway name changes to Karcher Road. Go 3 miles from the end of the ramp on Karcher Road and turn left (south) onto Lake Avenue. After 5.5 accumulated miles turn right (west) onto Roosevelt Avenue and follow the signs to the visitor center. At the stop sign at Indiana Avenue (6.5 miles), turn left onto Upper Embankment Road, the main entrance to the wildlife refuge. Follow the road, turning right at 7 miles. Pass through the gate at the entrance to the visitor center. Park at the left (east) edge of the parking lot at 7.1 miles. The self-guided Nature Trail starts on the east end of the parking lot. GPS: N43 33.65' / W116 39.95'

The Hike

Allow time for enjoying the visitor center before you hit the Nature Trail; it will enrich your hiking experience. The center offers nature videos, bird identification tips, a spotting scope overlooking the lake, and a kids' activity area with nature puzzles and animal pelts.

In 2009 the 12,000-acre refuge turned one hundred years old. Designated a national wildlife refuge on February 25, 1909, by President Theodore Roosevelt, Deer Flat became one of the first national refuges in Idaho.

Prior to the development of the reservoir, named Lake Lowell, deer wintered in the area. The reservoir was built by constructing 40 miles of canal from the Boise River to dry land.

Deer Flat National Refuge includes a portion of Lake Lowell shoreline and more than one hundred islands on the Snake River. The National Wildlife Federation has certified Deer Flat as a wildlife habitat, and hikers will view a variety

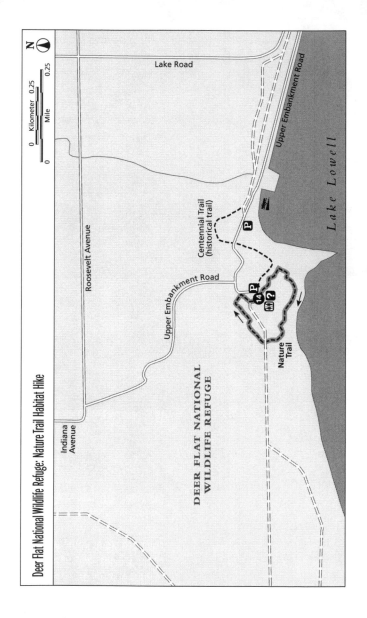

Deer Flat National Wildlife Refuge: Nature Trail Habitat Hike

N

0   Kilometer   0.25

0   Mile   0.25

Lake Road

Roosevelt Avenue

Indiana Avenue

Upper Embankment Road

Upper Embankment Road

Centennial Trail
(historical trail)

P

P

14

?

Nature
Trail

DEER FLAT NATIONAL
WILDLIFE REFUGE

Lake Lowell

of habitats on the short hike, including upland desert, wetlands, and a riparian forest lake.

Autumn and early winter are the best seasons for viewing a wide variety of wildlife. Winter bird migration begins in September. Bald eagles arrive in November. By December it is common for thousands of mallards and Canada geese to appear in the refuge. During spring, birds of prey settle in for nesting season.

Mornings and evenings, when the wildlife is active, are the best times to visit. Walk quietly and you might see or hear rabbits, squirrels, ospreys, meadowlarks, and kestrels. Cottonwood trees, cheatgrass, sagebrush, and rabbitbrush dominate vegetation along the trail.

Stop at the wildlife-viewing blind just off the trail, fondly nicknamed "The Coop." It is a gazebo-like structure where you tuck in to watch birds and animals as you remain unseen. Bird feed, bird identification posters, and wildlife-spotting opportunities make this a unique experience.

While at the reserve, checkout the newest addition—the 1.2-mile Centennial Trail, opened in 2009. This wheelchair-accessible historical trail starts near the visitor center. Additional access points are located at the east and the west boat ramp parking lots. Travel the paved trail and learn about the development of the refuge and the reservoir. A grant from the National Fish and Wildlife Foundation helped pay for the historic research, and a local college art student designed the interpretive signs.

Miles and Directions

0.0 Start at the sign marked NATURE TRAIL on the southeast side of the visitor center and head down the gently sloping trail. Within 465 feet arrive at the left-hand turn off the trail that leads a few hundred feet to the wildlife-viewing blind. To continue the hike, retrace your path and then turn left onto the Nature Trail.

0.4 Arrive at the intersection of a dirt road and the Nature Trail. Cross the road, continuing on the trail as it heads gently up a slope toward the parking lot. (**Option:** Detour on the 3.3-mile dirt road loop by turning left and accessing a wildlife-viewing platform overlooking the lake, located at 1.1 miles from this intersection.)

0.6 Arrive back at the trailhead. (**Option:** Explore the paved Centennial Trail, which starts at the east side of the parking lot at the Nature Trail trailhead.)

15 Boise National Forest: Mores Mountain Interpretive Trail Extension

For an alpine hike that features wildflowers in summer and colorful foliage in autumn, consider this nature trail in the Boise National Forest, 4 miles beyond the entry to Bogus Basin Mountain Recreation Area. The trail offers a bounty of sensory experiences and magnificent views of the valley and the distant mountain ranges.

Distance: 2.2-mile loop

Approximate hiking time: 2 hours

Difficulty: Moderate; steep, with loose rock on outer portion of the trail

Trail surface: Singletrack with dirt, sand, rocks, and pine needles

Best season: May through October

Other trail users: Pedestrians only

Canine compatibility: Leashed dogs permitted in the parking lot and campground area; off-leash dogs permitted on the trail

Fees and permits: Forest Service day-use fee

Schedule: The gate on the two-wheel-drive-accessible dirt Forest Service road (FS 374 E) is closed and locked from late October to late May. The gate by Frontier Point Lodge is closed during ski season, November through late April.

Maps: USGS Robie Creek; *DeLorme: Idaho Atlas & Gazetteer:* Page 35 C4; DeLorme Topo USA 7.0; Shafer Butte Trails—Ridge to Rivers map, available at outdoor retail shops throughout Boise or online at www.ridgetorivers.org; Boise National Forest Map, available from the Boise National Forest Supervisor's Office

Trail contacts: Boise National Forest, Mountain Home Ranger District, 2180 American Legion Blvd., Mountain Home 83647;

(208) 587-7961; www.fs.fed.us/
r4/boise; Ridge to Rivers Trail
System: (208) 514-3756

Supervisor, Boise National
Forest,1249 South Vinnell Way,
Boise 83709; (208) 373-4100

Special considerations: Mountain weather changes abruptly,
so be sure to dress in layers.
Refrain from picking wildflowers;
some may be rare plants.

Finding the trailhead: From I-84 take exit 53 and head north on
Vista Avenue. Go 2.1 miles to the intersection with Capitol Boulevard
and veer left onto Capitol Boulevard. Continue north on Capitol Bou-
levard to 3.1 cumulative miles and turn left (west) onto West Front
Street. Stay in the right lane and at 3.5 miles take the Front Street
exit. At 3.7 miles turn right (north) at the stop sign onto 15th Street.
Continue on 15th Street to 5.2 miles, arriving at the intersection with
Hill Road. Turn left onto Hill Road and proceed to the intersection
with Harrison Boulevard and North Bogus Basin Road (5.4 miles from
I-84). Reset the tripometer to 0. Turn right (north) onto North Bogus
Basin Road and travel for 16.1 miles to the entry of Bogus Basin
Mountain Recreation Area. Turn left off the paved road at the base of
the ski area; continue on the dirt road as it passes the Frontier Point
Lodge at 16.8 miles. At 19.6 miles turn right at the intersection.
Continue uphill on FS 374 E, entering the Shafer Butte Picnic Area
at 20.9 miles. Turn left and park in the day-use parking spots. GPS:
N43 47.05' / W116 05.15'

The Hike

Mores Mountain was named for one of the first miners to
discover gold in the Boise area during the 1860s. Located
at the base of Mores Mountain, the trail system consists of
three loops: an approximately 1.0-mile inner loop, a 1.3-
mile middle loop, and an outer loop extension totaling
2.2 miles round-trip. The following description covers the
outer loop extension.

The alpine trails described below were constructed by the Youth Conservation Corps in 1971 and 1975. Start by walking on a portion of the Mores Mountain Interpretive Trail. The trail sends hikers past two boulder-strewn granite outcroppings with wide-open vistas, including Shafer Butte (7,582 feet elevation). The 1.0-mile interpretive loop trail leads through meadows of purple, yellow, white, and red wildflowers; the middle loop trail leads to an overlook. Both connect with the end of the outer loop trail.

Hiking the outer loop extension entails traversing the dry and rock-strewn south-facing slope. After an uphill scramble on the rocky trail, follow the path as it contours near the base of Mores Mountain—at 7,237 feet, one of the highest peaks in the area. Views emerge of the national forest's undeveloped backcountry. Deer inhabit the open slopes below. The trail reconnects with the other two loop trails and descends through a deep old-growth forest with trees 100 to 125 years old. View the Sawtooth Mountains toward the end of this loop.

More than 200 plant and animal species live near the trail. Wild strawberries, syringa, sego lily, sticky geranium, penstemon, Indian paintbrush, and yarrow bloom at various times of summer. Flowering times vary depending on weather conditions.

Douglas fir trees dominate the area, although ponderosa pine, aspen, and mountain ash are common. Many of the larger Douglas fir trees are infected with dwarf mistletoe, indicated by pompom-shaped bushy branches at the crown of the tree.

Watch for wolf lichen attached to the bark of Douglas fir trees. It looks like bright green lace or hair. When wet, the lichen is soft and flexible; but during the dry season, it becomes dry and brittle. Fortunately, the lichen is not harm-ful to the trees.

Small owls, mountain bluebirds, woodpeckers, and nut-hatches nest in the standing dead trees called snags. Watch for chipmunks and gophers burrowing in the meadows. Hawks prey on these small animals.

Finish the hike with a picnic or barbecue at one of the day-use sites near the parking lot, or camp at the adjacent campground.

Miles and Directions

0.0 Start the hike at the northwest edge of the day-use area near the kiosk (6,721 feet elevation). Begin on the flat, log-lined trail used by bicyclists and equestrians. Continue for a few hundred yards, turning left at the first junction onto the pedestrian-only trail. This is the start of the Mores Mountain Interpretive Trail leading to the Mores Mountain Interpretive Trail Extension. Come to an outcrop viewpoint. Continue following the log-lined trail.

0.4 At the trail intersection, continue left for the Mores Mountain Interpretive Trail Extension. (**Option:** Turn right for the 1.0-mile loop.)

0.5 Arrive at outcrop and scenic overlook. Note Shafer Butte, the Bogus Basin Mountain Recreation Area's downhill ski slopes, Stack Rock, and the Treasure Valley.

0.6 Turn left (west) at the trail junction, accessing the Mores Mountain Interpretive Trail Extension. (**Option:** Turn right to continue on the middle loop.)

0.7 Turn right (northeast) at the small V in the trail. A large tree grew in the original trail, and a small footpath detours around the tree. In a few hundred yards turn left to rejoin the original trail, heading northwest.

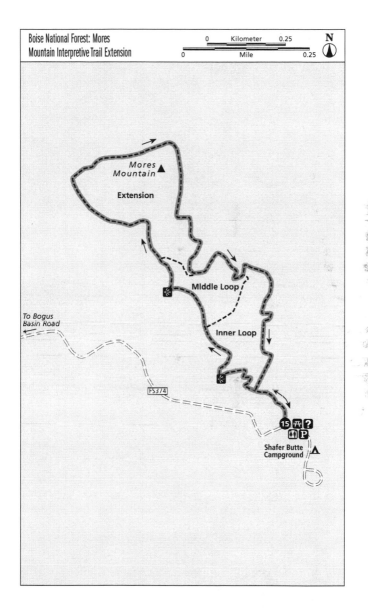

Boise National Forest: Mores Mountain Interpretive Trail Extension

Kilometer 0   0.25

Mile 0   0.25

N

Mores Mountain ▲

Extension

Middle Loop

To Bogus Basin Road

Inner Loop

FS374

15 🔤 ❓
🔣 P

Shafer Butte Campground ▲

0.9 The trail heads steeply uphill on loose rock. Crest the hill and move toward meadows at 7,164 feet in elevation. Pass near the base of Mores Mountain and through meadows.

1.2 Distant views of the Sawtooth Mountains come into view to the northeast. Continue on the trail through meadows then into brush and forest.

1.5 Arrive at the junction with the middle loop of Mores Mountain Interpretive Trail. Turn left (south) to continue on the outer loop.

1.7 The shorter loop, Mores Mountain Interpretive Trail, intersects the outer loop trail. Turn left, continuing on the outer loop.

1.8 Rest on the bench in the old-growth forest. Enjoy views of the distant Sawtooth Mountains and the nearby granite outcroppings.

2.0 Arrive at a junction with an unmarked trail. Turn right (south) toward the parking lot.

2.1 The trail intersects the starting point for the Mores Mountain Interpretive Trail system. Turn left (east) toward the aspen grove.

2.2 Intersect the bicycle/horse trail. Turn right to return to the trailhead, and arrive at the parking area in a few hundred feet.

16 Boise National Forest: Crooked River Trail

Walk through a high-elevation alpine ecosystem along a clear river on one of the few nonmotorized trails in Boise National Forest. Stunning rock outcroppings contrast with the surrounding forest. Smooth boulders in the waterway below the trail create small, steep rapids.

Distance: 2.6-mile out-and-back

Approximate hiking time: 1 hour

Difficulty: Easy; generally flat terrain with minimal elevation gain

Trail surface: Sand and dirt singletrack

Best season: May through October

Other trail users: Equestrians, mountain bikers, hunters (in season), and snowshoers

Canine compatibility: Unleashed dogs permitted

Fees and permits: No fees or permits required

Schedule: Year-round

Maps: *DeLorme Idaho Atlas & Gazetteer:* Page 35 B6; Boise National Forest map, available from the Boise National Forest Supervisor's Office

Trail contacts: Boise National Forest—Idaho City Ranger District, P.O. Box 129, Idaho City 83631; (208) 392-6681; www .fs.fed.us/r4/boise.

Supervisor, Boise National Forest, 1249 South Vinnell Way, Boise 83709; (208) 373-4100

Special considerations: During autumn hunting season, wear bright orange clothing. High water and river rapids are dangerous for swimmers. Do not remove any historical artifacts from gold dredge mining and timber production remnants or the Chinese miner enclaves that are part of the area's history. When fishing, follow catch-and-release requirement for bull trout.

Finding the trailhead: From I-84 take exit 54 (Broadway Avenue). Go north on US 20/26, locally called Broadway Avenue, for 3 miles to the intersection of Broadway Avenue, Idaho Street, Avenue B, and Warm Springs Avenue. Reset the tripometer to 0 and turn right (east) onto East Warm Springs Avenue. Go 7.5 miles to the intersection of East Warm Springs Avenue and ID 21. Turn left (north) onto ID 21 toward Idaho City. Continue on ID 21 past Idaho City to 56.9 miles cumulative to FS 384 (Crooked River Road). Turn right (east) onto FS 384 and drive past Edna Creek Campground. At 1.1 miles from ID 21, arrive at Crooked River trailhead. Park at the right (south) side of the road in the small pullout. GPS: N43 57.30' / W115 36.33'

The Hike

From the south side of the access road, begin the hike at 5,041 feet of elevation. A few hundred feet from the trailhead sign, the trail turns and meanders downstream along the Crooked River. Evidence of the area's gold placer mining history is visible along portions of the trail, indicated by piles of river rocks and stone remains of an old home. Private gold mining rights are still owned and mined along portions of the Crooked River.

During summer, sample fresh wild strawberries along the trail or fish for the huge bull trout that swim in the clear river below. Calm pools below rapids invite swimming on a hot summer day during lower water levels. Lodgepole pines are common along the banks of the river. Douglas fir and ponderosa pine stand tall on the slopes above the river. Be on the lookout for elk and mule deer during the hike.

Miles and Directions

0.0 Start at the pullout and head south down the hill off the edge of the road onto the Crooked River Trail (158). Cross

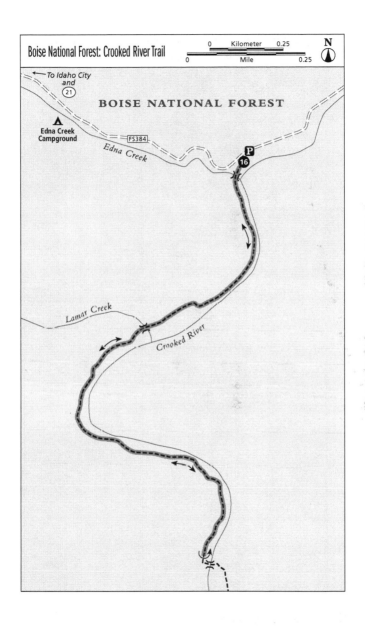

Boise National Forest: Crooked River Trail

0   Kilometer   0.25
0   Mile   0.25

N

← To Idaho City
and
21

BOISE NATIONAL FOREST

Edna Creek
Campground

FS384

Edna Creek

P
16

Lamar Creek

Crooked River

the wooden bridge over Edna Creek and then veer left. At 134 feet from the trailhead, the trail reaches the Crooked River's right (west) bank. Continue on the trail, paralleling the riverbank as the Crooked River flows downstream. Soon the trail moves slightly away from the river.

0.5 Reach a junction marked by a trail sign for Lamar Creek Trail, Lamar Creek Road, and Whoop-Um-Up Campground. Turn left (southwest) and cross the wooden bridge over Lamar Creek, continuing on the Crooked River Trail. Rejoin the Crooked River along its west bank. Granite outcroppings tower above the river.

1.1 The trail moves gently uphill as it parallels the boulder-strewn river and resulting rapids.

1.3 Arrive at the site of the new 70-foot-long single-span metal bridge over the Crooked River. This is your turnaround point. Return the way you came. (**Option:** Continue across the bridge to the river's east bank to access another 9.7 miles of trail. The additional trail is rated easy for another 2.5 miles before becoming increasingly rugged.)

2.6 Arrive back at the trailhead.

17 Bruneau Dunes State Park: Big Dune Hike

Ascend to the top of the largest single-formation sand dune in North America. From your elevated status on the dunes, you can view the distant Owyhee Mountains to the south, Flat Iron Butte to the north, Bennett Mountain to the north, and the lakes abutting the dunes. Watch jackrabbits race across open sagebrush desert and waterfowl feed in the sparkling lakes below.

Distance: 2.7-mile loop

Approximate hiking time: 1 hour

Difficulty: More challenging; loose, shifting sand and steep uphill climb

Trail surface: Sand, lots of it

Best season: March through May and September through November

Other trail users: The dunes serve as a makeshift sledding and ski hill year-round.

Canine compatibility: Leashed dogs permitted

Fees and permits: Motor vehicle day-use fee, payable at park entrance

Schedule: Year-round; daylight hours recommended. Directional disorientation can occur on the dunes at night.

Maps: *DeLorme: Idaho Atlas & Gazetteer:* Page 25 C6; DeLorme Topo USA 7.0; Bruneau Dunes State Park trail brochure, available at the visitor center

Trail contacts: Bruneau Dunes State Park, 27608 Sand Dunes Rd., Mountain Home 83647; (208) 366-7919; www.parks andrecreation.idaho.gov

Special considerations: Keep sand from migrating into socks and shoes by wearing ankle-high boots and long, loose pants that cover the shoes. If you have boot gators, consider using them. During spring and summer, bring water, bug spray, and sunscreen. The dunes are for nonmotorized use only. Temperatures can rise to 110 degrees Fahrenheit in summer, and the sand is hot. Strong winds blow frequently.

Finding the trailhead: From Boise take the Vista Avenue entry onto I-84. Go east on I-84 for about 38 miles to exit 90 (Mountain Home/Bruneau). At the end of the eastbound ramp, reset the tripometer to 0. Stay on I-84 Business toward Mountain Home for 3.5 miles to the junction of I-84 Business and ID 51. Continue straight on ID 51, going under the railroad overpass at 3.9 miles. Pass through two stoplights, heading out of Mountain Home on Airbase Road/ID 51. At 5.1 miles turn left, continuing on ID 51. After crossing the bridge over the Snake River, turn left at 19.2 miles onto ID 78 East. At 20.9 miles turn right onto Sand Dunes Road and the entrance to Bruneau Dunes State Park. Reach the self-service pay station at 21.8 miles. Continue past the visitor center, two campgrounds, the observatory, and the day use areas. At 24.6 miles the road dead-ends at the big lake parking area. Start the hike at the southwest edge of the parking lot. GPS: N42 53.73' / W115 41.90'

The Hike

The route described here is just one of many dune-hiking options on the Big Dune and smaller dunes in the area. This approach to the summit takes you up a steep slope and onto a saddle. At the saddle you can turn right and climb to the summit, 470 feet above the surrounding desert floor, or turn left and follow the razor-edge ridge running northeast. Other options are sliding, gliding, or striding directly off the flanks of the dune at any point.

During autumn and winter, the park's lakes serve as a stopover for migratory birds passing through the area. In addition to the transient birds, the park hosts songbirds and birds of prey.

Numerous habitats coexist in the park, ranging from desert prairie to marsh, and sand dunes to lakes. Many of the park's inhabitants are nocturnal. Note their tracks in the sand throughout the hike, and try your skills at identifying the tracks of kangaroo rats, lizards, beetles, deer, and coyotes.

This unique Idaho playground developed about 15,000 years ago. For dunes to form, a source of sand, constant winds, and a sand trap are needed. Bruneau Dunes State Park is in a semicircular basin that collected the silt, soil, and sand deposited by the Bonneville Flood. The flood created Lake Idaho, which eventually dried up and left behind the material the wind blew into the area. Winds keep the park dunes replenished and in place as they blow from two prevailing directions, southeast and northwest.

Create your own routes on any of the large and small dunes in the park. Several nearby smaller dunes make for less-challenging ascents and are popular with families with younger children. For an easy hike, consider the Little Lake Interpretive Trail.

Another major highlight of the park is the observatory. Far from cities and the resultant light pollution, the Bruneau Dunes Observatory is one of the largest public observatories in the Northwest.

Miles and Directions

0.0　Start at the southwest end of the big lake parking lot to the right of the boat launch area (2,481 feet elevation). Follow the gravel trail until it fades about 200 yards from the edge of the parking lot. Continue on the sand surface, with the lake to the left (south), following other boot prints paralleling the length of the dune.

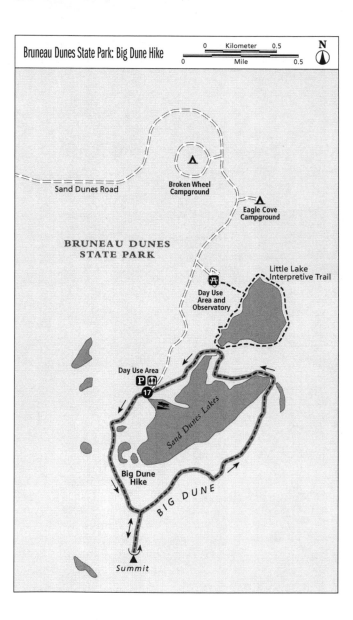

Bruneau Dunes State Park: Big Dune Hike

0 Kilometer 0.5

0 Mile 0.5

N

Sand Dunes Road

Broken Wheel Campground

Eagle Cove Campground

BRUNEAU DUNES STATE PARK

Little Lake Interpretive Trail

Day Use Area and Observatory

Day Use Area

P 17

Sand Dunes Lakes

Big Dune Hike

BIG DUNE

Summit

0.1 Turn south and head directly toward the dune, moving through brush, desert grass, and tiny dunes at the edge of the lake.

0.5 Start up the sand hill, heading toward the saddle of the dune.

0.7 Arrive at the top of the saddle between two high points on Big Dune (2,854 feet elevation). Turn right to continue toward one of the two highest parts on the dune. (**Option:** Turn left, continuing along the ridge then gradually down off the dune.)

0.8 Depart from first high point (2,938 feet elevation) and retrace your route back to the saddle. Note the waves of sand created by the wind and the small sand avalanches off the ridge edges initiated by your footsteps.

0.9 Return to the saddle and continue along the ridge, heading east. Look right (south) for a hawk's-eye view into the sand crater below. (**Option:** Head off the ridge at any time by retracing your route or heading left (north) steeply down to the base of the dune by the lake.)

1.1 The ridgeline starts gradually downward toward another saddle and up another, lower elevation hill on the ridge.

1.6 Head down the final hill leading to the flat land between the two lakes.

1.9 Arrive at a level area between the lakes. Veer left and walk through the brush.

2.0 Veer left and walk either along the shoreline (if the water level is low) or up above the brush line (if water is high), working your way along the north shore of the lake and heading west back to the parking lot. Keep the Big Dune to your left.

2.2 Walk through brush then slightly away from the lake on sand and amidst the brush.

2.7 Arrive back at the trailhead parking lot.

Hiking and Outdoor Clubs

Boise Women's Hiking Network (Boise WHN). This is an Internet-based hiking group geared toward women of various ages and fitness levels. For information contact Joyce Fabre at (208) 384-8582. Upcoming hikes are posted at http://groups.yahoo.com/group/BoiseWHN/.

Idaho Mountain Recreation. Conducts outings and education on the safe and responsible use of the outdoors. Call them at (208) 424-6683 or visit www.idahomountainrec.org.

Idaho Outdoors. Sign up for this online networking site to post announcements or join outings, including day hikes, extended backpacking trips, and other outdoor adventure activities at http://groups.yahoo.com/group/idahooutdoors/.

Mountain West Outdoor Club. One of the longest-standing outdoor clubs in the Treasure Valley, this year-round outdoor pursuits club offers member-led hikes and various other outings. Contact the club at (208) 323-1383 or join at http://groups.yahoo.com/group/MountainWest/.

Southwest Idaho Mountain Biking Association. Instrumental in trail developments projects in the Boise area, this mountain biking association is the group to contact for the insider's scoop on new and upcoming trail developments. Consider signing up for their volunteer trail-building and trail improvement projects. View information at www.swimba.org.

About the Author

A Pennsylvania native, Natalie L. Bartley moved to Idaho in 1987 for an outdoor program manager job after completing her doctorate in Parks, Recreation, and Leisure Services at the University of Utah. She has more than 800 magazine and newspaper articles to her credit, including a weekly outdoor column in the *Idaho Statesman*. She is also author of the FalconGuide *Best Rail Trails Pacific Northwest*.

Natalie is a certified kayak and ski instructor and a member of the Outdoor Writers Association of America and the Northwest Outdoor Writers Association. When not working as a freelance writer, she hikes, mountain bikes, whitewater kayaks, crosscountry skis, and explores the outdoors with her yellow Labrador retriever named Bruneau. She lives in Boise.